John Metham

Amoryus and Cleopes

Middle English Texts

General Editor

Russell A. Peck
University of Rochester

Associate Editor

Alan Lupack
University of Rochester

Advisory Board

Rita Copeland
University of Minnesota

Thomas G. Hahn
University of Rochester

Lisa Kiser
Ohio State University

Thomas Seiler
Western Michigan University

R. A. Shoaf
University of Florida

Bonnie Wheeler
Southern Methodist University

The Middle English Texts Series is designed for classroom use. Its goal is to make available to teachers and students texts which occupy an important place in the literary and cultural canon but which have not been readily available in student editions. The series does not include those authors such as Chaucer, Langland, or Malory, whose English works are normally in print in good student editions. The focus is, instead, upon Middle English literature adjacent to those authors that teachers need in compiling the syllabuses they wish to teach. The editions maintain the linguistic integrity of the original work but within the parameters of modern reading conventions. The texts are printed in the modern alphabet and follow the practices of modern capitalization and punctuation. Manuscript abbreviations are expanded, and *u/v* and *j/i* spellings are regularized according to modern orthography. Hard words, difficult phrases, and unusual idioms are glossed on the page, either in the right margin or at the foot of the page. Textual notes appear at the end of the text, along with a glossary. The editions include short introductions on the history of the work, its merits and points of topical interest, and also include briefly annotated bibliographies.

John Metham

Amoryus and Cleopes

Edited by
Stephen F. Page

Published for TEAMS

(The Consortium for the Teaching of the Middle Ages)

in Association with the University of Rochester

by

Medieval Institute Publications

WESTERN MICHIGAN UNIVERSITY

Kalamazoo, Michigan — 1999

Library of Congress Cataloging-in-Publication Data

Metham, John, fl. 1448.
   Amoryus and Cleopes / John Metham ; edited by Stephen Page.
      p.   cm. -- (TEAMS Middle English texts series)
   Includes bibliographical references.
   ISBN 1-58044-016-9 (alk. paper)
   1. Pyramus (Legendary character)--Romances--Adaptations.
   2. Thisbe (Legendary character)--Romances--Adaptations.
   3. Romances, English.   I. Page, Stephen, 1951-   .   II. Title.
   III. Series: Middle English texts (Kalamazoo, Mich.)
   PR2063.M34A8   1999
   821' .2--dc21   98-31520
                                                          CIP

ISBN 1–58044–016–9

Printed in the United States of America

Cover design by Linda K. Judy

Contents

Acknowledgments

Some of the ideas expressed here appeared in a different form in *The Chaucer Review* 33 (1996), 201–08. Richard H. R. Beadle, Gail McMurrary Gibson, and especially Lisa J. Kiser provided guidance and encouragement in the early stages of this project. In addition, I am grateful to Princeton University, which allowed me to examine and print this transcription from MS Garrett 141; I owe a special thanks to Don Skemer, Curator of Manuscripts, at Princeton's Firestone Library, for his efforts enabled me to read a portion of the last lines of the manuscript text of the poem with ultra violet light. This volume has been immeasurably improved by Russell Peck's careful reading and suggestions, and I am greatly indebted to him and also to his editorial assistant, Mara Amster, who checked my transcription of the text against a microfilm of the manuscript and formatted the volume. To my wife, Linda, who read parts of the Introduction and the Notes and who continues to inspire me every day, I owe my greatest debt of gratitude and my love. Special thanks go to the National Endowment for the Humanities for its generous support of the Middle English Texts Series.

For my Parents

Evelyn Herndon Page
William Scott Page

Amoryus and Cleopes

Introduction

The late medieval poem *Amoryus and Cleopes*, written by John Metham in 1449, survives in a single manuscript, Princeton University Library's MS Garrett 141. The poem is the longest and central piece in the manuscript, which includes several medieval scientific/philosophical treatises, also by Metham: two sets of prognostications, one based on the day on which Christmas falls and the other based on the days of the lunar cycle; a guide to palmistry; and a guide to human character based on physiological characteristics. Garrett 141, although not a lavish or large manuscript, was nevertheless carefully produced on vellum and decorated with relatively large floriated initials at the beginning of its longest works. The whole volume is written in a single hand, an Anglicana Formata with a high number of Secretary features. The details of this paleographic mix and certain idiosyncrasies of spelling (discussed below) suggest that the copying of Garrett 141 was some decades removed from the original composition date of *Amoryus and Cleopes*. The whole manuscript was carefully and ornately rebound in the seventeenth century.

Amoryus and Cleopes has been almost totally neglected by modern scholarship since it was first edited by Hardin Craig in 1916.[1] This neglect can be explained by a number of factors, including perhaps primarily the poem's often chaotic metrics, but also the biographical obscurity of the poet as compared to other fifteenth-century poets; the limited number of extant works by the author; the general deprecation of English poetry, as compared to that of the Scottish poets like Henryson, Dunbar, and Douglas in the fifteenth and early sixteenth centuries; and the generic mix of the poem, combining elements of classical myth, medieval romance, and religious miracle. However, revisionist historical evaluations of fifteenth-century English literature now see that literature as important for our understanding of Chaucer's own works. How his works were read and interpreted by his near contemporaries has become a central focus of Chaucerian scholarship in the last two decades. Metham's poem, in fact, can be seen as a key piece in the reception of Chaucer's works, coming just at the time of the death of John Lydgate, Chaucer's most prolific fifteenth-century English follower, and before the rise of Scottish Chaucerians. *Amoryus and Cleopes*, in fact, adopts Chaucer's tone and borrows details of scenes and

---

[1] See Select Bibliography for the complete reference.

narrative strategies from Chaucer's Ovidian tales, such as that in *The Book of the Duchess*, and especially from his romance-epic masterpiece, *Troilus and Criseyde*. The poem furthermore does not slavishly use these features of Chaucer's compositions but adapts them to Metham's own ultimately moral purpose, fusing them with elements of classical tale, courtly and popular romance, encyclopedic compendium, hagiography, mirror for princes, and encomium, to create a tightly constructed late-medieval romance.

The Author and His Patrons

The Garrett MS and a version of Metham's treatise on palmistry in All Souls College, Oxford, MS 81 are all that survive of Metham's works. No documentary sources other than these two manuscripts refer to him as a writer. The last ten lines of *Amoryus and Cleopes*, erased from the manuscript but now partially visible under ultraviolet light, provide a number of biographical details — which Metham seems to have been interested in promulgating — about his aristocratic ancestry.

According to the manuscript, Metham was born in Cambridge, although his father had been born in the "north cuntre," undoubtedly Yorkshire, where the village of Metham was located. The manuscript further claims that poet's father was by "right consanguinity" descended from "the first Alexander Metham, the knight." This is almost certainly Sir Alexander Metham (1375–1417), who as head of the Metham family in Yorkshire owned seventeen manored estates and other lands in that county. Although Sir Alexander's father, Sir Thomas Metham III (1332–1403), had earned distinction in the French wars, the few extant historical records concerning Alexander are all of a local nature and suggest a country gentleman tending to his inherited wealth. Sir Alexander's heir was Sir Thomas Metham IV (1402–72), but Sir Alexander had another son, also named Alexander, whom our poet distinguishes from the elder when he writes "the first Alexander Metham, the knight." The first son, Sir Thomas IV, who in 1443 and 1460 was Sheriff of Yorkshire, married and had his first son about 1420. According to a family pedigree, Thomas had five sons, including a younger son named John.[2]

If we believe the poet's claim of "right consanguinity," that is, legitimate and direct descent from Sir Alexander Metham, then this younger son of Thomas and the poet John Metham are perhaps one and the same. Although his birth in Cambridge instead of

---

[2] For the Metham family in Yorkshire, see P. Saltmarshe, "Some Howdenshire Villages," *Transactions of the East Riding Antiquarian Society* 16 (1909), 1–49; K. J. Allison, ed., *A History of the County of York: East Riding*, vol. 4, The Victoria History of the Counties of England (London: Oxford University Press, 1979), p. 23; and Robert Glover, *The Visitation of Yorkshire, Made in the Years 1584/5 . . . 1612*, ed. Joseph Foster (London: Joseph Foster, 1875).

Yorkshire remains unexplained, the dates of the poet's active period correspond with the age one of Thomas' younger sons could have attained at the mid-point of the fifteenth century. The poet tells us he is writing *Amoryus and Cleopes* in 1449, which would place our candidate in his twenties. The poet writes in his palmistry treatise, included in the same manuscript, that he is in the twenty-fifth "wyntyr of hys age."

About Metham's education little more can be said. In the scientific treatises of the Garrett MS, the poet refers to himself as a "simple scholar of philosophy" and a "scholar of Cambridge," but his translations of these treatises from the Latin, as Craig notes, are often awkward, and if he were indeed at some time a student at the university, Craig's surmise that he was not one at the time of writing and was trying to remember his Latin in relative isolation seems probable. Because there are no records of him at the University during the fifteenth century, it is possible that the reference to himself as a "scholar of Cambridge" refers to his place of birth rather than the fact that he was attending the university at the time of composition.[3]

Metham's patrons, fortunately, are well documented in historical records. Sir Miles Stapleton (d. 1466) was one of the leading men of Norfolk during the middle part of the fifteenth century.[4] In 1427 he was appointed to care for the signal beacons in Norfolk to warn of French invasions during the Hundred Years' War. He later served in France, having license from the French for safe passage to transport prisoners for ransom in 1436–37 and again in 1441. In 1440 he was Sheriff of Norfolk and Suffolk, and the next year he was Knight of the Shire and summoned to Parliament and to attend the King's Council. He again served as member of Parliament in 1448 and 1450. In addition, he was appointed by the King to serve on a number of commissions to raise funds and muster troops in Norfolk and Suffolk for the English war effort. He was also appointed to help maintain a local militia to resist any seaborn attack by the French, and served on numerous Commissions of the Peace to investigate lawlessness and to bring to justice wrongdoers in Norfolk.

---

[3] A John Metham was a resident of Cambridge in 1418 when he was "ill-used" by the clerics of the University. His relationship to the poet, if any, has yet to be determined. See Charles H. Cooper, *Annals of Cambridge*, 5 vols. (Cambridge: Cambridge University Press, 1842–53), I: 162. In his *A Biographical Register of the University of Cambridge to 1500* (Cambridge: Cambridge University Press, 1963), A. B. Emden accepts the notion advanced by Craig that Metham wrote *Amoryus and Cleopes* at about the time he was in the twenty-fifth "wyntyr of hys age" and so assigns his birth date to c. 1423.

[4] For the Stapleton family in Norfolk see James Lee-Warner, "The Stapletons of Ingham," *Norfolk Archaeology* 8 (1882), 183–233; Walter Rye, *Norfolk Families* (Norwich: Goose and Son, 1913), pp. 844–46; and The Public Record Office, *Calendar of the Patent Rolls Preserved in the Public Record Office: Henry VI, A.D. 1422–1461*, 6 vols. (Public Records Office, rpt. Nendeln, Liechtenstein: Kraus, 1971), especially vol. 4 for 1441–46, passim.

Sir Miles married twice, first to Elizabeth Felbrigge, who died without bearing children, and second, to Katherine de la Pole, who bore two daughters as heirs. The first wife, Elizabeth, was the daughter of Sir Simon Felbrigge (1368–1442), and, like Stapleton himself, a prominent landowner, frequently involved in public affairs and also in foreign campaigns. Katherine de la Pole, Metham's patron whom he praises at the end of the poem, was the daughter of Sir Thomas de la Pole, uncle of one of the great magnates, William, Duke of Suffolk, oldest son of Michael de la Pole, the Earl of Suffolk.

The Stapletons of Ingham represent a southern branch of an aristocratic family that had, like Metham — and about which I will say more shortly — originally come from Yorkshire.[5] The great grandfather of our poet's patron, another Sir Miles Stapleton of Bedale, Yorkshire (d. 1364), had an illustrious career in the wars in France, participating in the great English victory at Crécy, and was one of the original Knights of the Garter.[6] His second marriage was to the daughter and sole heir of Sir Oliver Ingham, Joan, who brought a considerable Norfolk estate into the Yorkshire family. Their eldest son was also Sir Miles (d. 1419), who married the niece of Robert Ufford, Earl of Suffolk. Their heir, Sir Brian (c. 1379–1438), married the daughter of William, Lord Bardolf, who became Sheriff of Norfolk. Brian was taken prisoner in the French wars, and ransomed, in part, by war-rich neighbor Sir John Fastolf of Yarmouth, Norfolk.

Given the propensity of aristocratic and gentry families to arrange marriages with local families with whom they had similar landed interests, it not surprising that the Yorkshire families of the Methams and the Stapletons had ties of kinship. Elizabeth, the second cousin of the Garter Knight Sir Miles Stapleton, married Sir Thomas Metham III in 1370; their heir is Sir Alexander Metham, mentioned above, perhaps the grandfather of the poet. As a consequence of this marriage, a considerable amount of land that had been in the Stapleton family came into possession of the Metham family. What then seems probable concerning the relation of the two families and the poet John Metham is that after he attended Cambridge, he sought employment with his relatives in Norfolk, and joined the Stapleton retinue where he may have had administrative duties in the household or perhaps in the attached Trinitarian Priory founded in 1360 by the Stapleton family. In the concluding *envoy* of *Amoryus and Cleopes*, Metham encourages the reader to seek his four other major works — all now lost — to find biographical encomia about his patrons, Sir Miles and Lady Katherine. He then proposes to continue to write about Miles Stapleton's

---

[5] For the Yorkshire branch of the Metham family and its relationship to the Ingham branch, see Joseph Foster, *Pedigrees of the County Families of Yorkshire*, vol. 1: *The West Riding* (London: W. Wilfred Head, 1874), [n.p.]

[6] See Lee-Warner, "The Stapletons of Ingham," p. 200; and *Dictionary of National Biography*.

many heroic deeds. Both his previous writings and the prediction, or perhaps supplication, suggest that Metham had been regularly compensated by the family. We may speculate that Metham was either a sometime-poet living in Norwich, or perhaps, more likely, a member of the Stapleton retinue, perhaps the family secretary.

The Poem and Its Literary Relations

The core of Metham's medieval romance is an adaptation of the Pyramus and Thisbe story from Book 4 of the *Metamorphoses* of Ovid (43 B.C.–A.D.18), Metham substituting the names Amoryus and Cleopes, respectively, for those of the hero and heroine of the classical tale.[7] Ovid's story is one of tragic love similar to Shakespeare's *Romeo and Juliet*: Pyramus and Thisbe are forbidden to see one another by their parents. The lovers nevertheless manage to express their love during clandestine meetings at a crack in the stone wall that separates their parents' estates. Speaking through the fissure in the wall, they agree to rendezvous secretly outside the town under a mulberry tree at the site of Ninus' tomb. Thisbe arrives first at the appointed place, but a lion forces her to flee, and in her flight, she drops a scarf. The lion, fresh from a kill, wipes its bloody maw on the scarf, then ambles away. Pyramus, finding the cloth, believes Thisbe has been eaten by the lion, and in grief kills himself with his sword under the mulberry tree. Returning from her hiding place, Thisbe finds Pyramus dead and commits suicide with Pyramus' sword. The metamorphoses occurs when Pyramus' spurting blood turns the white mulberry red, a permanent color transformation.

This Ovidian tale was adopted for Latin grammar schooling in the twelfth century, and it thus became, during the later Middle Ages, one of the most widely read works from the *Metamorphoses* and, indeed, from all classical Latin literature.[8] In the same century, Ovid's poem was considerably amplified in the French romance *Piramus et Tisbé*, which was later borrowed in its entirety for inclusion in the fourteenth-century French *Ovide Moralisé*. This anonymous poem and a concise Latin prose rendering of Ovid's version in the *Ovidius Moralizatus* by the Benedictine monk Pierre Bersuire (c. 1290–d. 1362) additionally provided allegorical commentaries on Ovid's *Metamorphoses*. Consequently, these two works provided Christian significance — and therefore sanction by Church

---

[7] See Ovid (Ovidius Naso), *Metamorphoses*, 2 vols., third ed., ed. and trans. Frank Justis Miller, rev. G. P. Goold, Loeb Classical Library (Cambridge, MA: Harvard University Press, 1984), 2:182–91.

[8] See E. H. Alton and D. E. W. Wormell, "Ovid in the Medieval Classroom," *Hermathena*, 94 and 95 (1960 and 1961), 21–38 and 67–82.

officials — to Ovid's secular, pagan stories. In the allegorization of the Pyramus and Thisbe story, for example, Pyramus is interpreted as a figure of Christ, Thisbe as the Virgin Mary, and the Lion as the Devil, and in this guise the legend became an exemplum in sermons.[9] Several fourteenth-century English versions of the classical tale or its medieval moralization further disseminated it among readers in the fifteenth century. These include renderings by Chaucer in his *Legend of Good Women*, one of his most frequently copied works, by John Gower in the *Confessio Amantis*, and by Christine de Pisan in the *Épitre d' Othéa*, translated into English by Metham's contemporary and fellow Norfolkian, Stephen Scrope.[10] The version most widely known to modern audiences is the burlesque play presented by Bottom and the other "mechanicals" in Shakespeare's *A Midsummer Night's Dream*.

Amoryus and Cleopes is, like the French *Piramus et Tisbé*, a medieval reworking of the classical story into a romance. Originally, the word *romance* simply meant a work in one of the vernacular languages descended from Latin, rather than Latin itself, but the term came to be identified with a certain type of fictional work that may be defined (usually) as the adventures of a knight. Romances developed their characteristic features in the twelfth century, and from A.D. 1150 to about 1450, they were among the most common

---

[9] Raymond Cormier, ed. and trans., "Piramus et Tisbé," in *Three Ovidian Tales of Love*, Garland Library of Medieval Literature, vol. 26, series A (New York and London: Garland, 1986), pp. 3–83. C. De Boer, ed., "Pyramus et Thisbé," *Ovide Moralisé: Poème du Commencement du Quatorzième Siècle*, 5 vols. (Amsterdam, 1915–38), 2:18–41. The *Ovidius Moralizatus* comprises the fifteenth book of Bersuire's *Reductorium Morale*; see the facsimile of the 1509 printed edition of the *Reductorim*, entitled *Metamorphosis Ovidiana Moraliter . . . Explanata*, ed. Stephen Orgel (New York: Garland, 1979), Liber IV, fol. xxxvii; G. R. Owst, *Literature and Pulpit in Medieval England*, second ed. (Oxford: Blackwell, 1966), pp. 179–80.

[10] Chaucer further mentions the story in the *Parliament of Fowls* (line 289) in the context of one of the mural paintings of tragic love stories in the Temple of Venus; in The Man of Law's Tale (line 63) in the catalogue of Chaucer's works; and in The Merchant's Tale (lines 2825–31) as an exemplum of love's determination. (Line numbers refer to *The Riverside Chaucer*, third ed., ed. Larry D. Benson, et al. [Boston: Houghton Mifflin, 1987]; all further citations of Chaucer's works refer to this edition.) Gower's tale is an exemplum of foolish haste; see *Confessio Amantis*, ed. Russell A. Peck, Medieval Academy Reprints for Teaching 9 (Toronto: University of Toronto Press 1966; rpt. 1980), pp. 176–80. For Scrope's rendering of the story, see *The Epistle of Othea*, XXXVIII, ed. Curt F. Buhler, EETS o.s. 264 (London: Oxford University Press, 1970), pp. 49–51. In addition, John Lydgate is reputed to be the author of a brief version of the story; see Ernst Sieper, ed., *Lydgate's Reason and Sensuallyte*, EETS e.s. 84 (London: Oxford University Press, 1901; rpt. 1965), pp. 104–05. (Sieper's studies and notes to the poem appear as a separate volume, EETS e.s. 89 [London: Oxford University Press, 1903; rpt. 1965].) William Caxton's own translation and personal copy of the *Metamorphoses* (no printed copies survive) contains an illustration of the legend as a headpiece to Book 4; see *The Metamorphoses of Ovid Translated by William Caxton, 1480*, vol. 1, Books 1–9, The Phillipps Manuscript (New York: G. Braziller, 1968).

and widespread type of fictional narrative in western Europe. In England, the earliest extant romance dates to c. 1225, and the total number of extant Middle English romances composed before the end of the fifteenth century numbers about 115, though certainly many others have been lost.[11] Like their continental counterparts, the English romances vary greatly in the type of material which the authors include. In addition to knightly activities, any given romance may contain — with differing degrees of emphasis — a heroine and a love interest for the knight, or it may lack a heroine altogether. It may display "courtoisie" and chivalric deeds, marvels and miracles, incidents which question or reinforce feudal and social relationships and obligations, and religious and ethical concerns, though not necessarily. And there are romances like *Lay le Freine* in which a woman is the central figure and chivalric deeds are entirely absent. Because medieval authors considered all texts to be tacitly unfinished, authors could expand or abbreviate a received text to whatever extent and to whatever purpose they might choose. For example, as is well known, Sir Thomas Malory extensively reworked the French sources of his *Morte D'Arthur*, often eliminating introspective, psychological passages and the mystical symbolism of the French cycle, and partly as a consequence, accentuating action and morality in his English redaction. Metham, instead of condensing Ovid's already brief tale of Pyramus and Thisbe, has, like the twelfth-century romancer of the *Piramus et Tisbé*, considerably expanded the legend. In doing so, he gives wider scope to most of the features of romance adduced above: chivalry, courtly love, and Christian morality all become central concerns of this now thoroughly medievalized story.

Metham begins *Amoryus and Cleopes* with a brief historical description of the Roman emperor Nero's conquest of the kingdoms of Persia and Media. Two Roman lords, Palamedon and Dydas, the fathers of Amoryus and Cleopes respectively, are awarded control of the two realms. The narrative then turns quickly to the marvelous. Conjuring spirits with demonic magic, the chief priest of the Temple of Venus creates a mechanical marvel, a sphere that replicates the medieval cosmos; after completing the sphere, he has prophetic dream visions that warn of the downfall of the Roman gods. The love theme advances to the foreground of the romance when, at the rededication of the temple (earlier destroyed by an earthquake), Amoryus and Cleopes see each other for the first time. His new-found love motivates Amoryus in a chivalric tournament celebrating the new temple, and he defeats all competitors, including a discourteous knight whose armor presents a fantastic array of heraldic devices. The poem then returns more directly to the courtly love story that parallels the Pyramus and Thisbe tale, the lovers discovering the chink in the

---

[11] The number derives from a cursory count of the list of romances in J. Burke Severs, gen. ed., *A Manual of the Writings in Middle English, 1050–1500*, vol. 1: *Romances* (New Haven: Connecticut Academy of Arts and Sciences, 1967), pp. 13–16; see also R. M. Wilson, *The Lost Literature of Medieval England*, second ed. (London: Methuen, 1970), pp. 104–34.

wall and offering ardent affirmations of their love. In the ensuing episode, chivalry, aristocratic responsibility, and the quest for fame take precedence over love when Amoryus suddenly volunteers to fight a dragon which is devastating a nearby kingdom. He of course singlehandedly defeats the dragon, but Cleopes helps prepare him and insures his victory. The final element of the romance merges chivalric and courtly romance with Christian miracle. The two lovers agree to meet outside of the city, and commit suicide just as Pyramus and Thisbe do. However, unlike Ovid's characters, Metham's two dead lovers are resurrected by the prayers of a hermit who discovers their bodies. Along with the revived lovers, the hermit returns to town and exorcizes the demonic spirits from the sphere at the same time as pagan images are destroyed and the gods themselves are exposed as fraudulent and expelled. The citizens are converted to Christianity, and Amoryus and Cleopes are married by the anchorite performing the Christian sacrament.

Metham's romance owes some of its inspiration to the popular romance tradition, and an important component in this group of romances in the late Middle Ages was the life and wars of Alexander the Great, one of Nine Worthies. Metham's reference to his lost work *Alexander Macedo* at line 2144 (see notes) indicates he was familiar with at least one version of an Alexander romance, and, as Craig noted, *Amoryus and Cleopes* does borrow details from Alexander legends.[12] Battles between Alexander and Darius over the rule of Persia comprise a significant series of episodes in the longer Alexander stories; these episodes are recalled in the setting of Metham's poem, which takes place in Persia. And through the marriage of their Roman fathers with Persian noble women, Amoryus and Cleopes become descendants of Darius. In the romance *King Alisaunder*, Neptanamous, Alexander's natural father, is a magician; so too in Gower's *Confessio Amantis*.[13] In *King Alisaunder* he creates a "table," or engraved surface of gold, that displays the stars so that through necromancy and astronomy he may know "the goddes pryvete."[14] A similar device

---

[12] See Craig, pp. xiii–xv. R. M. Lumiansky's claim in "Legends of Alexander the Great" (in *A Manual of the Writings in Middle English*, 1:112) that it borrows "numerous details" overstates the case, but the comment has been focused on by almost every later writer who mentions the poem. Metham's interest in Alexander stories may have been stimulated by his relationship to Sir Alexander Metham. For an overview of the medieval Alexander literature in England, see Gerrit H. V. Bunt, *Alexander the Great in the Literature of Medieval Britain*, Mediaevalia Groningana, no. 14 (Groningen: Egbert Forsten, 1994).

[13] See *Confessio Amantis*, Book 6, lines 1789–2366, for the "Tale of Nectanabus," where Alexander, upon hearing that his teacher will be killed by his son and not knowing that he was fathered by the magician, throws him off a wall to prove his teacher wrong, thus fulfilling the prophesy. Gower's Nectanabus performs numerous amusing magical feats.

[14] G. V. Smithers, *King Alisaunder*, EETS o.s. 227 (London: Oxford University Press, 1952), lines 133–38, and 262. Further references to this edition will be made parenthetically in the text.

is described later in the poem as Alexander comes upon it in Tripoli at the Temple of Termagaunt and Balat (two devilish idols):

> On ymage was therin,
> Ybeten al with gold fyne,
> Sonne, and mone, and steorren seven
> Was therein purtreyed, and hevene. (1509–12)

Neptanamous is comparable to Venus' secretary in *Amoryus and Cleopes*, who likewise is a necromancer, able to summon spirits to create his celestial sphere, which, however, is described in considerably more detail than the device in the Alexander romance. It is possible, too, that one of the characters' names (King Albanyen, line 5261) or one of the places mentioned (the Kingdom Albyenne, line 7944) in *King Alisaunder* gave rise to the name of the capitol of city of Metham's Persia, Albynest. In another Alexander romance, *The Wars of Alexander*, an image of Xerxes is mysteriously destroyed: "It all topaschis into peces & to poudire dryuys" (It entirely shatters into pieces and is reduced to powder); in *Amoryus*, images of the gods in the Temple are also "smet to poudyr" (line 119).[15] But the suggestion for this phrasing may equally have come from a romance on the legend of Joseph of Arimathea, in which Joseph encourages a heathen to do away with his idols, "breken hem a-two and bren hem al to pouder."[16]

Though other details drawn from Alexander romances might be elucidated, it would be more valuable to acknowledge Metham's debt to other sources, including the general body of popular romance. The hero and heroine of *Amoryus and Cleopes* are in many ways typical of these romances. They are aristocratic and young. Amoryus is courageous, kind to his inferiors, and "able to rule a realm"; Cleopes is beautiful, clever, and provides aid to save Amoryus. Certain events in *Amoryus and Cleopes* come straight from this popular tradition.[17] For example, Amoryus' love at first sight of Cleopes, and their later exchange of rings are commonplaces in Middle English romances, motifs derived from folk tales. Amoryus' fight with the dragon puts him in a league with a host of other dragon fighters, including such popular English romance heroes as Guy of Warwick and Bevis of

---

[15] Hoyt N. Duggan and Thorlac Turville-Petre, eds., *The Wars of Alexander*, EETS s.s. 10 (Oxford: Oxford University Press, 1989), lines 5304–48.

[16] Walter W. Skeat, *Joseph of Arimathie: Otherwise Called The Romance of the Seint Graal*, EETS o.s. 44 (London: N. Trübner & Co., 1871; rpt. 1992), line 103.

[17] Often the events and themes in romances derive ultimately from folk-tale motifs. See Gerald Bordman, ed., *Motif-Index of the English Metrical Romances*, F(olklore) F(ellows) Communications, no. 190 (Helsinki: Academia Scientiarum Fennica, 1963).

Hampton. Guy kills two dragons, one of which, like the *serra cornuta* that Amoryus chooses to face, is devastating a neighboring country. Bevis of Hampton has as one of his goals to marry the heroine, Josian, and one of many impediments he encounters is the dragon of Cologne. Bevis' fight and his own invocation of St. George were clearly intended to make Bevis into a "Christian champion." Amoryus, although a pagan who has no concept of marriage, has a union with Cleopes as his goal and also chooses to face a dragon, which he likewise defeats. Another key element in the romances concerns the pledging and testing of *trwth* (troth), meaning loyalty or fidelity. Although *trwth* often concerns relationships between knights, or between knights and their lord or servants and their masters, it is also always a topic at issue in the relationships of men and women in the romances; and in all three cases, the pledging *trwth* is a pledge to remain loyal even to the death, should it be required. So it is in *Amoryus*. When the two protagonists plight their troth to serve and love one another (lines 1117–34), the issue immediately becomes whether they will remain loyal. Their later suicides are the epitome of pagan and misguided *trwth*, but this expression of loyalty only serves to deepen their love and commitment to one another (lines 1926–32).

Some critics have chosen to call the romance a "mode" or "form" rather than a "genre," and do so because of the romance's capacity to accommodate so many other types of literature. A cursory survey of the Middle English metrical romances may reveal, by turns, fictional battle stories, quasi-historical chronicles, lyrics, moral exempla, sermons, quasi-saints lives, the latter types encompassing explicitly religious events. The miraculous, as distinguished from the inexplicably marvelous, occurs in a significant number of religiously oriented English romances. For example, in *Amis and Amiloun*, God orders two children to be put to death so that their blood may heal a leper; the leper is healed and both children are found alive and sound the following day. Similarly, a stillborn child in the romance of *The King of Tars* is miraculously revived as a healthy boy after his baptism. In the romance *Athelston*, a falsely accused queen wife walks unscathed across red-hot plowshares, aided by God, and proves her fidelity. *Amoryus and Cleopes*, like these and a good proportion of other English romances, presents a didactic and explicitly religious story. Like *Amis and Amiloun*, the religious element is evident in the resurrection of the two protagonists, a resurrection achieved through the intercession of the wandering Christian anchorite, Ore, who represents the antithesis of the Venus' secretary. By resuscitating and subsequently officiating at the marriage of the two lovers, Ore brings them into the Christian community, and, like the protagonists of many romances, the two recover what has been lost, in their case, life, love, and, ultimately, patrimony. *Amoryus and Cleopes* also resembles a saint's life, for not only are the two protagonists resurrected in imitation of Christ, but Amoryus' dragon fight puts him in a typological relationship with St. George, who is, of course, a type of Christ.[18] Furthermore, the hero and heroine's devotion to one another and their (perhaps accidental) chastity makes them proper candidates for the resurrection miracle and conversion. In addition, *Amoryus and Cleopes* presents a Christian conversion story. Not only are the two lovers converted, but also, on the evidence of Amoryus' and Cleopes' miraculous revival, the citizens likewise abandon their misguided beliefs and embrace the new religion. Even Palamedon, who early in the story adamantly rejects worshiping a "hanged man," is brought into the Christian community. Similar conversions, whether mere episodes or central plot features, occur often in English romances, and in such diverse works as the crusading Charlamagne romances *The Sultan of Babylon* and *The Siege of Milan*; the legend of the English hero, *Sir Bevis of Hampton*; *St. Erkenwald*, where the old pagan man of the law is miraculously converted during the reconstruction of the temple by one teardrop from the priest; or the Griselda-Constance story of the calumniated woman in *The King of Tars*. In the latter, the miraculous baptism persuades the king to convert and to enforce conversion on his kingdom.

In spite of similarities it shares with popular romances, *Amoryus and Cleopes* also lacks a host of motifs that are stock features of romances: noticeably absent are giants, dwarves, mistaken identities, disguises, magic swords or girdles, good or bad stewards, the recovery of disposed inheritance, and so on. One might reasonably compare Metham's Ovidian tale to the fourteenth-century poem *Sir Orfeo*, another medievalized tale from the *Metamorphoses*. Unlike the narrator of the *Orfeo*, Metham's narrator refuses to suggest an oral recitation or oral reception, but rather comments frequently on the written source from which he works, a source which distances the poem from the popular romances of the thirteenth and fourteenth centuries. Although there is magic in *Amoryus and Cleopes*, it is an effect of the natural properties of things, or a demonic magic that is invoked and explicable rather than spontaneous and mysterious like the faerie magic of *Sir Orfeo*. Nor does *Amoryus and Cleopes* disguise its characters, test their feudal loyalty, or abduct them to the faerie world: except for the visitation of Venus and the priest's invocation of spirits, Metham's characters operate in a real, if idealized, world. Furthermore, Amoryus and Cleopes are well schooled in courtly manners and the observances and pains of courtly love. Although love occurs in many of the popular English romances, like *Bevis*, the rough and ready characters of many chivalric romances seldom devote much attention to the niceties of *amour courtois* or *courtoisie* as they do in *Sir Gawain and the Green Knight* or the romances of Chaucer. Metham's work is also more tightly constructed than most other longer Middle English metrical romances: an earthquake leads to both the rebuilding

---

[18] Bevis of Hampton even invokes the name of St. George to make the point explicit. Other English romances that read like saints' lives include *The Earl of Toulouse*, *Le Bone Florence of Rome*, and *Amis and Amiloun*.

of the Temple, where the lovers first see one another, and also to the creation of the hole in the wall through which they communicate. The rededication of the Temple prompts the making of the diabolical sphere, which indirectly leads to the priest's dream vision, forecasting the downfall of the Roman gods at the end of the romance. The dedication of the temple is also the cause for the celebration of the tournament in which Amoryus proves his courage and prowess at arms, in turn making him a creditable opponent for the dragon.

When Metham departs from the Middle English popular romance tradition, he does so in the direction of the more elite type of poetry which owes its inspiration, like much other fifteenth-century English poetry, to Chaucer's works. Like Chaucer, Metham's immediate audience was a group of well-educated people, that is, his patrons and other aristocrats and gentry in the Stapletons' circle who held similar interests in literature. Consequently, it is not surprising that Metham's poem blends elements of popular romance with aspects of Chaucer's *romans antique* (The Knight's Tale and *Troilus and Criseyde*), his composite romance (The Squire's Tale), and his courtly love poetry in the early dream visions.[19] Judging by the numbers of extant manuscripts, these poems were among Chaucer's most frequently copied works in the fifteenth century; and it was these poems and his love lyrics — rather than his "more realistic" *Canterbury Tales*, such as The Miller's Tale — which most attracted fifteenth-century readers and amateur poets. As Seth Lerer has pointed out, these Chaucerian poems provided the "rules of formation for poetry" in the fifteenth century, and Metham was abiding by those rules (p. 11).

At one level of indebtedness, Metham quotes, paraphrases, or recasts the language of the *Troilus*, and orders his narrative in a manner similar to Chaucer's. The use of Chaucerian language is immediately evident in Metham's imperfect adoption of the rhyme royal stanza (not the meter) and in the phrasing of the first seven lines of *Amoryus and Cleopes*, which are clearly intended to remind the reader of the initial lines of *Troilus and Criseyde*; Metham writes:

> The chauns of love and eke the peyn of Amoryus, the knygt,
> For Cleopes sake, and eke how bothe in fere
> Lovyd and aftyr deyd, my purpos ys to endyght.
> And now, O goddes, I thee beseche of kunnyng, that Lanyfyca hyght:
> Help me to adornne ther chauns in sqwyche manere
> So that qwere this matere dotht yt reqwyre,
> Bothe ther lovys I may compleyne to loverys dysyre.

---

[19] On the *roman antique*, see Barbara Nolan, *Chaucer and the Tradition of the Roman Antique* (see Select Bibliography); on the composite romance, see Jennifer R. Goodman, "Chaucer's *Squire's Tale* and the Rise of Chivalry," *Studies in the Age of Chaucer*, 5 (1983), 127–36; and Kathryn L. Lynch, "East Meets West in Chaucer's The Squire's Tale," *Speculum* 70 (1995), 530–51, especially 546–47.

This stanza, like that of Chaucer's Prologue to Book I (see Notes, lines 1–7) promises a double movement, first to love and joy and then to sorrow and death. Just as Chaucer employs the classical machinery of invoking his muse, Thesiphone, one of the Furies, so Metham invokes Lanyfyca (from Latin, relating to the *weaving of wool*), another name for the Fates who controlled a person's destiny by spinning, weaving, and cutting the thread of life. Chaucer's *Troilus*, with its prologues, text, and envoy at the end of Book V, initiates a structural formula which was to become the standard and expected pattern of longer fifteenth-century poetic works. Not surprisingly, Metham appears to have intended *Amoryus and Cleopes* to have a similar structural division of four books (instead of five) followed by an envoy. The manuscript marks prologues for the First, Third, and Fourth Books, and large capital letters indicate other possible divisions missed by the scribe. Similarly, Metham employs another fifteenth-century commonplace, a conclusion which becomes at once the conventional apology for his poor verse and a lament for the makers of poetry, Chaucer and John Lydgate (?1370–1449), Chaucer's most prolific and influential disciple.

There are many other parallels with Chaucer's *Troilus*. Metham's narrator is clearly modeled on Chaucer's: a clerkish, humanist translator who works from a classical source by a fictitious author, here Fyrage instead of Lollius. The two narrators both fail to acknowledge the true source of the core story, Boccaccio and Ovid, and both are expressly sympathetic to the hero and heroine. At the beginning of Metham's story, Amoryus, like Troilus, is untouched by love; when Amoryus first sees Cleopes in the Temple of Venus, in a scene very closely modeled on that in which Troilus and Criseyde first see each other, he is immediately smitten.[20] *Amoryus and Cleopes* differs most noticeably from the plot of the *Troilus* in its happy, miraculous resolution to the story. Not only does this comic conclusion subvert the expectations of the reader, expectations raised by the Ovidian tale and Metham's adaptation of first stanza of the *Troilus*, it also functions as commentary on Chaucer's tragic tale and the supposedly inviolate authority of sources, and represents a kind of blending of Chaucer's classical *romans antique* with some of the techniques of his earlier dream visions. As in Chaucer's other Ovidian tales, such as the story of Seyes and Alcyone in *The Book of the Duchess*, or Chaucer's own rendition of the Pyramus and Thisbe story in his *Legend of Good Women*, Metham does not include Ovid's metamorphosis, in this case the transformation of color on the mulberry. Chaucer's habit in the earlier works, it would seem, provided Metham with a model of authorial freedom that allowed him to do what he wished with the conclusion to Pyramus and Thisbe.

---

[20] On Metham's debt to Chaucer's model narrator, see my article, "John Metham's *Amoryus and Cleopes*" (see Select Bibliography).

Amoryus and Cleopes

The story and Metham's handling are also reminiscent of other Chaucerian works. As in the *Canterbury Tales*, a knight and his son go on a pilgrimage in which the travelers entertain one another with "myry songys and talys day be day" (line 405). Like The Knight's Tale and the *Troilus*, *Amoryus and Cleopes* foregrounds the mannered love of "courtoisie," which in the English romances before Chaucer is the exception rather than the rule. Metham's protagonists meet clandestinely simply because the conventions of courtly love demand that love be secret, not because, as in Ovid, they are forbidden to see one another. Furthermore, after their first sight of one another, the lovers succumb to the pains of romantic love-sickness and emote their feelings in stereotypical ways, but not unlike the courtly dalliance of Chaucer's characters. In some ways, too, like The Squire's Tale, *Amoryus* shows an interest in natural magic and astrology, subjects that at the time were associated with the Orient, an interest that is manifest in Alexander stories as well; but, as indicated above, the poem is well constructed, and it lacks a number of other features of the composite romance type.

One of the notable features of Metham's romance is its comedy, and the nature of that comedy owes a considerable debt to Chaucer's early dream poems. Metham burlesques the dream vision in the appearance of the goddess Venus to her priest. Instead of a divine vision of love or sensuality, Venus appears as a weeping, distraught figure, remarkably ungodly. The vision of the goddess becomes ridiculously physical when she, according to the priest, began "[p]unchyng me with her fote" (line 664). The secretary, like some of Chaucer's dull narrators, apparently does not believe or understand the dream, causing the goddess to return to repeat her message in another dream. Such broad humor seems to be inspired by scenes from Chaucer's dream poetry. In *The Parliament of Fowls* (line 154), the indecisive dreamer/narrator is shoved through a gate by his dream guide; in *The Book of the Duchess*, a spirit messenger must awaken the god of sleep, Morpheus, by blowing "his horn ryght in [his] eere" (line 182). The narrator's comic encounter with the great eagle in *The House of Fame* comes very close to Metham's scene: the eagle grasps the timid narrator with its "fet" and tells him to "Awak!" (Bk 2, 554 ff.). Some of the humor seems more generally stimulated by Chaucerian poetry. For example, after revealing the remedies against the dragon to Amoryus, Cleopes directs him to get the required precious stones from the jeweler, Walter, a very pedestrian business for a knight and perfectly in keeping with Chaucer's frequent exploitation of the incongruous for comic effect. This is not to suggest, however, that *Amoryus and Cleopes* is a thoroughgoing parody of popular romance, like The Squire's Tale or The Tale of Sir Thopas; rather, it maintains a finely balanced tone between the comic scenes and its ultimately serious and didactic purpose, which would be completely undermined by characters too ignoble and ludicrous for conversion.

It is this comic tone that distinguishes Metham's work most from that of John Lydgate, whose serious and moral tales never achieved, or perhaps never attempted, the light comic touch which Metham achieves in *Amoryus and Cleopes*. Certainly Metham knew Lydgate's works and derived some of his ideas directly from them. For example, as has been discussed above, Cleopes aids Amoryus in his fight with the dragon, giving him an antidote against its venom and instructing him in the use of a ring she had earlier given to him. This is closely paralleled in Lydgate's *Troy Book*: Medea aids Jason in his quest for the Golden Fleece by providing him with an ointment that protects him from fire-breathing bulls and a ring set with a green stone for use against a dragon.[21] But whereas Lydgate narrates the scene between Jason and Medea, Metham puts Cleopes' directions to Amoryus and his response in energetic dialogue and develops the comic possibilities of the scene. Metham also derives the destruction of the pagan statue of Venus and the marvelous sphere from a passage in the *The Troy Book*. Lydgate relates a similar story of a statue of Apollo — like Metham's Venus, inhabited by a fiend and destroyed at Christ's birth. But whereas Lydgate's narration is merely the springboard for a long digression on the origins of idolatry, Metham's version is dramatically presented and fully integrated into the whole romance.

Metham is no Chaucer: His syntax, especially in the more astronomical material, can be difficult. His use of aureate (that is, Latinate) terms in imitation of Chaucer and Lydgate is sometimes awkward, again, primarily in the astrological sections. And in reading Metham's descriptive passages on astronomy and the gods, one has the feeling of, as in reading Lydgate's romances, tedium. However, the astronomical and astrological materials that Metham elaborates on were popular topics, as witnessed by other manuscripts possessed by the Stapleton family (see below). Moreover, on the whole, Metham's vocabulary is surprisingly modern and readable, and like Chaucer — but diametrically opposed to Lydgate — Metham avoids turning events and characters into excuses for digression and moral diatribes. When Metham is at his best — in his use of dialogue, in crafting of a coherent narrative out of a host of sources and genres, in developing and maintaining a deft comic tone, in understanding and using the Chaucerian narrator to contrive a new ending for the Pyramus and Thisbe legend — he approaches Chaucer's narratives in some ways better than many other poets in the first half of the fifteenth-century.

Metham's allusion to *Troilus and Criseyde* in the first stanza of his poem invites, as discussed above, a comparison of his narrative technique with that of Chaucer; it also invites comparisons with Chaucer's versification and stanza patterning. Evaluations of the prosody of the romance have been especially negative, one critic calling the poem "almost

---

[21] John Lydgate, *Lydgate's Troy Book, A.D. 1412–20*, 3 vols., ed. Henry Bergen, EETS e.s. 97, 103, 106, 126 (London: K. Paul, Trench, Trübner & Co., 1906), Bk. 1: 2996–3074, and 3260–3357. Further references will be cited in the text.

unreadable" because of, in part, its apparent metrical ineptitude.[22] A cursory glance at *Amoryus* would seem to confirm this position. The reader may note in the first stanza widely divergent line lengths, some exceeding Chaucer's regular decasyllabic line by as many as seven additional syllables. Furthermore, although some lines may be rendered iambic, such as lines one and two by elision of syllables in the names of the protagonists, most lines have neither a consistent metrical pattern nor do they evidence a regular stress like that of English alliterative poetry. Metham's lack of attention to versification is nowhere more apparent than in the embedded lyric comprising lines 381–401. Although the poet twice refers to the lyric as a "song(e)" (lines 380, 402), which suggests it should have regular metrical patterning, its verses are as variable in syllabic count and as rhythmically diverse as the lines of the first stanza of the poem.

Such obvious inattention to prosody is unusual among fifteenth-century courtly poets, most of whom at least tried to imitate Chaucer's verse. Although criticism may be leveled at the poet for his lack of metrical sense, we may also conclude that he was simply not interested in prosody, that his real concern was an effective narrative. As is well known, narratives like *Amoryus and Cleopes* were usually intended to be read aloud, and Middle English metrical romances often suggest the circumstances of oral performance, as Metham does in line 1059, where he uses the word "spake" instead of "wrote." As indicated by the encomium that concludes his poem, Metham was writing for an aristocratic audience similar to that envisioned in the famous illumination in Corpus Christi College, Cambridge, MS 61, which depicts Chaucer orally presenting his *Troilus* to a courtly audience. If *Amoryus and Cleopes* is evaluated by the criterion of oral performance, it does not disappoint: the problem of the metrics becomes relatively unimportant, and what strikes the ear is a fluid and nuanced rhymed prose.[23]

As is also evident from a cursory glance at MS Garrett 141, Metham has written his poem mostly in seven-line stanzas, each new stanza being marked by the scribe with an initial large capital letter that readily stands out from the smaller capitals that mark the

---

[22] The comment, with which I and other readers strongly disagree for reasons discussed below, is made by Derek Pearsall, "The English Romance in the Fifteenth Century," *Essays and Studies* 29 (1976), p. 69 (see Select Bibliography). See Benson, *Riverside Chaucer*, pp. xlii–xlv, for an overview of Chaucer's versification.

[23] On the nature of fifteenth-century prosody and stanza forms in general, see H. S. Bennett, *Chaucer and the Fifteenth Century*, Oxford History of English Literature (Oxford: Clarendon Press, 1947), pp. 129–30; and see also the Introduction to *English Verse Between Chaucer and Surrey*, ed. Eleanor Prescott Hammond (Durham: Duke University Press, 1927), especially pp. 21–24; her introduction also provides a succinct overview of the period. Although scholarship has acknowledged oral performance as a feature of Middle English poetry, it has only been within the last few years that such performances have been advocated in order to fully appreciate the poems.

beginnings of the following six verses. This seven-line stanza, rhyming *ababbcc*, has its origin in Chaucer's rhyme royal stanza used in *The Parliament of Fowls, Anelida and Arcite, Troilus and Criseyde*, and the tales of the Man of Law, the Clerk, the Prioress, and the Second Nun. The rhyme royal, or, to name it more accurately for Chaucer's successors, the "Chaucer stanza," was profoundly influential on fifteenth-century poetry and was employed both in fictional and practical literature, including treatises on husbandry and economic policy. Almost all of Lydgate's work, including his own *romans antiques*, *The Troy Book* and *The Siege of Thebes*, adopt it, as do two anonymous fifteenth-century popular romances, the *Romauns of Partenay* and *Generydes*.[24] Although *Amoryus and Cleopes* is normally regular in its use of the Chaucer stanza, the poem's first stanza immediately signals a tendency to diverge from the model. Almost all of the variations in the poem are patterned *ababacc* (28 stanzas) or *abaabcc* (18 stanzas). Occasionally, stanzas are either six lines (13 stanzas) or eight lines (9 stanzas). Sometimes six- and eight-line stanzas are juxtaposed on the same page of the manuscript, apparently to justify the length of the pages, which are always ruled for twenty-eight lines, or four Chaucer stanzas (see lines 759–71, 926–40, 1108–20, and 2185–99). Particularly telling in this regard are two stanzas comprising lines 759–71, in which, in the manuscript, a nonsense line is used to complete an eight-line stanza and fill out the last line on the page (see Notes, line 771). [In addition there are two sets of couplets (lines 246–47 and 1346–47), and a sequence of three six-line stanzas comprising part of Cleopes' excited disquisition about the types of dragons (lines 1263–80).] For an elevated rhetorical effect, the poet uses a single rhyme for the first six lines in one eight-line stanza (lines 1989–96, rhyming *aaaaaacc*), in which the a-rhymes are all aureate words in *-io(u)n*. Such attentions indicate that the author is indeed concerned with prosody, if not meter.

The love lyric mentioned above deserves special attention, for although Sir Thomas Wyatt has been universally credited with writing the first sonnet in English, Metham's lyric remarkably anticipates any other extant fourteen-line poem in English by at least eighty years. Overlooked by previous readers of *Amoryus and Cleopes*, the sonnet itself is embedded within a double narrative frame. The first frame consists of a journey from Rome to Albynest of Amoryus, his father, and their entourage, during which the young men decide to sing a song of love. The song presents the second narrative frame in which

---

[24] On the name of the stanza, see Martin Stevens, "The Royal Stanza in Early English Literature," *PMLA* 94 (1979), 62–76; and on its use by Chaucer, see Barry Windeatt, *Troilus and Criseyde*, Oxford Guides to Chaucer (Oxford: Oxford University Press, 1992), 354–59; see also H. S. Bennett's and Eleanor Prescott Hammond's works cited above. One of the two extant versions of *Generydes* is written in the Chaucer stanza and occurs in a lavish manuscript produced for another important Norfolk family contemporary with the Stapletons; see Derek Pearsall, "Notes on the Manuscript of *Generides*," *The Library*, fifth ser., 16 (1961), 205–10.

a speaker, "I," recounts the story of his morning walk and of his overhearing a lover complaining to Fortune about the loss of his lady (lines 381–87), a complaint which the speaker reiterates and which forms the sonnet proper (lines 388–401):

> "'O, Fortune! Alas! qwy arte thow to me onkend?
> Qwy chongyddyst thow thi qwele causeles?
> Qwy art thow myne enmye and noght my frend,
> And I ever thi servant in al maner of lovlynes?
>
> "'But nowe of my lyfe, my comfort, and my afyauns
> Thowe hast me beraft; that causyth me thus to compleyn.
> O bryghter than Phebus! O lyly! O grownd of plesauns!
> O rose of beauté! O most goodely, sumtyme my lady sovereyn!
>
> "'But, O, allas! that thru summe enmye or sum suspycyus conjecte,
> I throwyn am asyde and owte of my ladiis grace.
> Sumtyme in faver but now fro alle creaturys abjecte
> As oftyn sqwownyng as I remembyr her bryght face.
> But now, adwe for ever, for my ful felycyté
> Is among thise grene levys for to be.'"

The lament is clearly presented as a sonnet in the manuscript (fol. 24a): its two quatrains, like other stanzas in the manuscript, are marked with large initial capitals, and are the only examples of quatrains in the poem. With the following six-line stanza, the embedded sonnet has a rhyme scheme of *abab cdcd efefgg* and therefore also anticipates the form of the sonnet which Henry Howard, Earl of Surrey, has been credited with originating and which Shakespeare was to later adopt for his sequence.[25] The thought pattern does not exactly coincide with the stanzas, but there is a general sonnet-like organization of ideas into two parts: the lover first complains to Fortune about some unspecified mischance in the first six lines, then in a series of apostrophes, fills out the "octave," hinting that the

---

[25]Athough none of Surrey's poems are adaptations of Metham's sonnet, it is quite possible that Surrey — whose father was Thomas Howard (1517–47), third Duke of Norfolk — could have seen the manuscript. The Howards had extensive landholdings in Norfolk and Suffolk, including main palaces at Kenninghall and Framlingham, where Surrey is buried, and a townhouse in Norwich. Although a manuscript which contains an English sonnet and a comic rendition of the Pyramus and Thisbe legend is extremely tantalizing, none of Shakespeare's sonnets are derived from Metham's (though, as with Metham's relation to Petrarch, they share commonplaces of the European love lyric); and a burlesque of the legend, so widely taught in Latin grammar schools, can hardly have been unique.

cause of the distress concerns the speaker's "sumtyme . . . lady sovereyn." That cause is explicitly revealed at the beginning of the "sestet" where the lover reveals he has fallen from his lady's favor due to slander. After returning to the idea of his unfortunate fall and his own physical decline in swooning, the speaker concludes with a couplet, a coda signaling his resignation to be forever among the green leaves (rather than with the flowers associated with the lady).

How did Metham come to compose the first English sonnet so long before its development and flourishing in the sixteenth century? We can only speculate. The form, as is well known, had originated in thirteenth-century Sicily and was subsequently taken up by Italian poets, including Dante, in his *Vita Nuova*, and Petrarch, who greatly extended its range and flexibility in his *Canzoniere*. Both poets were, of course, mentioned by Chaucer in his works, thus familiarizing many English readers with their names. Chaucer, however, appears not to have had firsthand knowledge of the *Vita Nuova*, and although he did translate one of Petrarch's sonnets in his *Troilus* (I:400–20), he rendered it in three rhyme royal stanzas and did not provide an attribution. A possible source of Metham's model for the form was an early manuscript of Petrarch's poems in the library of Peterhouse at Cambridge by 1426[26]; however, the sonnet does not translate any poems from either *Vita Nuova* or the *Canzoniere*. Because Metham's fourteen-line poem diverges so much from the rhyme scheme, thought, and imagery of Petrarch's poems, if he did encounter Petrarch's sonnets during his matriculation at Cambridge, they were incompletely remembered, and necessarily adapted to the relative difficulty of rhyming in English as opposed to rhyming in Italian.[27] The general situation of the whole song — a lover's complaint overheard — is much more strongly reminiscent of Chaucer's *Book of the Duchess* and Lydgate's later *Complaint of the Black Knight* than of any Italian predecessor. And the language and subject matter of the sonnet itself are commonplaces of medieval love poetry stemming from Ovid and the lyrics of the *troubadours* and *trouvères* of France and taken up by the sonneteers: the distant lady, love rejected, malicious gossip, and the anguished lover. The apostrophes about lost love faintly echo

---

[26] James Bass Mullinger, *The University of Cambridge*, 2 vols. (Cambridge: Cambridge University Press, 1873–84), 1: 433, cited in Lewis Einstein's *The Italian Renaissance in England* (New York: B. Franklin, 1962), p. 54.

[27] Craig (p. xi) has noted that Metham's Latin in his other works in the Garrett MS also has a quality of being only partially remembered. Metham's sonnet does share themes with Petrarch's sonnets, for example, poems 172 and 274 *(Petrarch's Lyric Poems: The* Rime Sparse *and Other Lyrics*, ed. and trans. Robert M. Durling [Cambridge, MA: Harvard University Press, 1976], pp. 318–19, 452–53), but these similarities are, as I indicate below, part of the common poetic idiom of Western Europe.

Troilus' much longer complaint (IV.260–336), where Fortune is also "unkynde" (line 266). The comparisons of the lady to the lily, the rose, and the sun on the one hand, and the love-lorn man's confinement to the green-leaved forest on the other may be an allusion to an episode in *The Roman de la Rose* or perhaps to the courtly May Day game and poetic motif debating the relative merits of the flower and the leaf.[28]

The Social and Literary Context

As suggested above, it is likely that Metham was connected to the Stapleton household in some capacity. As one of the leading men in the area, active in local political and military endeavors, Sir Miles' household and entourage must have been appropriately opulent.[29] The manor at Ingham was subjoined to a priory of Trinitarian friars, a foundation established in 1360 by the first Sir Miles Stapleton to settle in Norfolk, and our fifteenth-century Sir Miles owned six other manors — four in Norfolk, one in Suffolk, and one in Yorkshire — as well as a townhouse in Norwich.[30] All of this far flung land would have required a sizable staff of literate overseers and personal attendants for the Stapleton family, no doubt including a secretary. In addition to local activities on Commissions of the Peace, Commissions of Muster, and as sheriff of the county, Stapleton was a member of the prestigious religious Guild of St. George in Norwich. Most religious guilds were

---

[28] For *The Complaint of the Black Knight*, see *The Minor Poems of John Lydgate*, vol. 2, ed. Henry Noble MacCracken, EETS o.s. 192 (1934; rpt. Oxford: Oxford University Press, 1961), 2: 382–410. Lydgate's poem is also heavily dependent on *The Romance of the Rose*, for which see *The Romaunt of the Rose and Le Roman de la Rose: A Parallel-Text Edition*, ed. Ronald Sutherland (Berkeley: University of California, Berkeley, 1968), especially lines 3011–82 in the *Romaunt* and lines 2823–964 in the *Roman*, where Bialacoil, Fair Welcoming, gives the lover a leaf from the rose bush, but both characters are in constant danger from a number of other allegorical figures, including Malebouche, a scandal monger who concocts injurious stories. For the flower and leaf debate, see Derek Pearsall, ed., *The Floure and the Leaf, The Assembly of Ladies, The Isle of Ladies* (Kalamazoo: Medieval Institute Publications, 1990); and Chaucer's *Legend of Good Women* (line F 72, and n., p. 1061).

[29] On the court culture of the later Middle Ages and the necessary opulency of noble households, see Richard Firth Green's stimulating book, *Poets and Princepleasers*, especially pp. 15–16 (see Select Bibliography).

[30] W. H. Cook, Norfolk Public Record Office, Norwich; Ms. COL/8/81/1–4. The townhouse was in the parish of St. Julian, where the famous recluse St. Julian of Norwich was enclosed. For the priory, see also, T. J. Pestell, "Ingham Priory (Norfolk)" in Margaret Gray's "The Trinitarian Priory of Thelsford, Warwickshire," *British Archaeological Reports*, (1992).

parochial institutions, but the Guild of St. George drew its membership from all over East Anglia and included such magnates as the Bishop of Norwich, the Duke of Suffolk, and Sir John Fastolf — one of the richest men in England — as well as Stapleton's first father-in-law, Sir Simon Felbrigge, and members of the Paston family.[31]

Stapleton's library must have been a substantial one because the display of books was another way of indicating one's standing in the hierarchy of late medieval society. In addition to the romance and the other astronomical and physiognomical material in the Garrett MS, Metham indicates a number of other works he had written for the Stapletons. The *Alexander Macedo* has already been discussed, but the envoy of *Amoryus and Cleopes* also indicates that Metham had written several more works, one called *Josue*, presumably a reworking of the story of Joshua from the Old Testament, a work called *Josepus*, which could refer to a number of different subjects, and *Crysaunt*, possibly a treatise on husbandry by Petrus de Crescentiis (see notes to lines 2144–45 and 2170). In addition to these works, two other volumes are extant from the Stapleton library. The first of these is Oxford Bodleian Library, MS Bodley 758, a copy of the *Vita Christi* (The Life of Christ) by Michael de Massa. This vellum manuscript containing the Stapleton arms was, according to the scribe, copied in 1405 at Ingham (probably in the priory) for Sir Miles Stapleton (d. 1419), the grandfather of our Sir Miles. Since such books were relatively expensive they tended to be heirlooms and were passed down to family members; it is likely that this manuscript was still in the Stapleton library in the mid-fifteenth century. The second book is a version of *The Secret of Secrets*, called *The Privyté of Privyteis* in the manuscript, translated for Sir Miles Stapleton by the otherwise unknown Johannes de Caritates. Ostensibly a series of letters between Alexander the Great and his tutor Aristotle, the *Privyté* is a work in the "mirror for princes" tradition, a handbook for governing and self-governance, but also containing medical information, a physiognomy, and instructions for creating the Philosopher's Stone, an alchemical treatise. This manuscript was copied by the same scribe who copied the works of John Metham in the Garrett MS.[32] The *Vita Christi* and the *Privyté* were fairly common works in the libraries of late medieval English noblemen, and in the case of Stapleton, they compare to the literary and intellectual tastes revealed in the Garrett MS and to manuscripts or books owned by his elite Norfolk contemporaries, like Sir John Fastolf and Sir John Paston. The

---

[31] Francis Blomefield and Charles Parkin, *An Essay Towards a Topographical History of Norfolk*, second ed. 11 vols. (London: William Miller, 1805–10), 3:349–50. See also David Galloway, ed., *Norwich, 1540–1642*, Records of Early English Drama (Toronto: University of Toronto Press, 1984), pp. xxvi–xxix.

[32] The *Privyté* has been edited by M. A. Manzalaoui, in *Secretum Secretorum: Nine English Versions*, EETS o.s. 276 (Oxford: Oxford University Press, 1977), pp. 114–202. See also Richard Beadle, *Prolegomena* p. 103, #36; p. 105, #77; and p. 106, #106.

Vita Christi is a biblical harmony of the Gospels, and such books were relatively common among the clergy, as were compilations of saints' lives and moral tales. These were a little less common among the aristocracy and gentry, but almost every member of the gentry and nobility would have had a primer, a book of hours, or a psalter (though few had Bibles in English, which were outlawed in 1408). Fastolf's library included a French Bible, a copy of the *Meditations of St. Bernard*, as well as a number of other liturgical books in his private chapel at his castle at Yarmouth.[33] Such a collection is consonant with late medieval piety, which on the evidence of wills, church donations, and the explosion of religious guilds in the fifteenth century, was devout and sincere. Such devotion also accords with the dragon fight in *Amoryus and Cleopes*, which is at once religious and hagiographical and also celebrates the guild to which Stapleton belonged. The resurrection of the pair and their conversion is furthermore part of what has been called the "incarnational aesthetic" of late medieval religion, that is, the tendency to "formulate concrete images" of Christ and those whose lives imitate his, the saints.[34]

Of course, Stapleton's neighbors among the wealthy gentry and aristocracy of East Anglia read and patronized other types of literary production. Fastolf's household maintained an active literary coterie of writers and translators who developed a "secular outlook similar to that of the humanist scholars of Italy," and Stephen Scrope, Fastolf's stepson, translated Christine de Pisan's *Epistle of Othea* about 1440, at the request of Fastolf.[35] In addition, Fastolf owned French copies of the *Book of King Arthur*, *The Romance of the Rose*, and *The Brute*.[36] Elsewhere, we have the well-known bibliophilic disposition of John Paston II, whose famous list of his English books includes not only his own copy of Scrope's translation *Epistle of Othea* but also several Middle English popular romances, the *Death of Arthur*; *Guy of Warwick*; *Kyng Richard, Couer de Lion*; and a version of *Sir Gawain and the Green Knight*. Paston also owned several works of Chaucer, including *The Legend of Good Women*, *The Parliament of Fowls*, and *Troilus and Criseyde*.[37] In fact, East Anglia figures prominently in the early history of the transmission of the works of Chaucer. In their discussion of the provenance of manuscripts

---

[33] See H. S. Bennett, *The Pastons and Their England*, p. 111 (see Select Bibliography).

[34] See Gail McMurray Gibson, *The Theater of Devotion*, pp. 1–18, and 67–106.

[35] Jonathan Hughes, "Stephen Scrope and the Circle of Sir John Fastolf," especially p. 133 and p. 146 (see Select Bibliography).

[36] H. S. Bennett, *The Pastons and Their England*, p. 111.

[37] Norman Davis, ed., *The Paston Letters and Papers of the Fifteenth Century*, 2 vols. (Oxford: Clarendon, 1971–76), 1:517–18. Members of the family also owned copies of Lydgate's *Temple of Glass* and *The Siege of Thebes*.

of *The Canterbury Tales*, Manly and Rickert claim a number of pre-1450 copies originated in the region, including the famous Ellesmere MS, containing portraits of the pilgrims. This manuscript's early history is clearly connected with an area on the Essex/Suffolk boarder near Bury St. Edmunds, and it may have been for a while in the hands of members of the Paston family.[38] Ellesmere was furthermore a model for another important early Chaucer manuscript from East Anglia, Cambridge University Library MS Gg.4.27, which like the Ellesmere MS contains portraits of the pilgrims. Dating from about 1415–20, this manuscript is important for two reasons: it "translates" Chaucer's London English into the provincial forms of East Anglia, and it represents the earliest attempt to collect all of Chaucer's works into one volume, including as it does several of the *Tales*, *The Legend of Good Women*, *The Parliament of Fowls*, and *Troilus and Criseyde*.[39] Two other manuscripts of the *Troilus* also have their provenance in East Anglia and date from the second quarter of the century, London, B.L. MS Additional 12044, and Durham, University Library, MS Cosin V.iii.13, two closely related manuscripts. This early connection of East Anglia with the production of Chaucer manuscripts is a complicated and still evolving story, but for our purposes here we need look no further than Chaucer's granddaughter, Alice, who had in 1430 married William de la Pole (d. 1450), one of the great magnates of the first half of the fifteenth century, himself a poet and patron of John Lydgate. William's uncle, Thomas de la Pole, was the father of Stapleton's second wife, Katherine de la Pole, and the armorial insignia of both families are combined in a large heraldric shield placed on the first page of *Amoryus and Cleopes*. Sir Miles and Lady Katherine Stapleton lived in a social and cultural milieu which patronized literary production, and their association with owners of Chaucer manuscripts, even if they themselves did not possess any, must be undoubted. Metham's own access to such manuscripts seems equally certain.[40]

---

[38] John M. Manly and Edith Rickert, *The Text of the Canterbury Tales* (1940; rpt., Chicago: University of Chicago Press, 1967), 1:501–02; Ralph Hanna, III, and A. S. G. Edwards, "Rotheley, the De Vere Circle, and the Ellesmere Chaucer," *Huntington Library Quarterly* 58 (1996), 11–35. Other early manuscripts of the *Canterbury Tales* from East Anglia include B.L. Add. MS 35286 (Suffolk); Princeton University Library MS 100 (from the library of Helmingham Hall, Suffolk), and Holkham Hall (Norfolk) MS 667.

[39] M. B. Parkes and Richard Beadle, eds., *Poetical Works: Geoffrey Chaucer — A Facsimile of Cambridge University Library Ms. Gg.4.27*, 3 vols. (Norman, OK: Pilgrim Books, 1979–80), 3: especially pp. 1, 3, and 54.

[40] Samuel Moore's article, "Patrons of Letters in Norfolk and Suffolk, c. 1450" (see Select Bibliography), focuses on the patronage of East Anglian writers such as Lydgate, Bokenham, Capgrave, and Scrope and suggests the close relationships of their patrons.

The Language and Date of the Manuscript

The language of the poem is fifteenth-century East Anglian. Infinitives of verbs are usually uninflected or end in *-e*, although a few infinitives in *-n(e)* also occur as rhyme words, *deyn* (line 1757), *seyn* (lines 1116, 1563), and *fordone* (line 1781). In the present indicative, the first person forms are uninflected or end with *-e*; the second person forms end in *-st*, except for *wotys* (line 360), which results from sound elision with the following pronoun *thow*. Third person forms typically end in *-th*, although *-t* (*nedyt* line 165; *hat* lines 372, 979) and *-tht* (*dotht* lines 6, 1351; *seytht* line 80; *ferytht*, line 1345) also occur. The scribe has written almost all plural verbs with no ending or *-e*, with the exception of two verbs ending in *-n*, *arn* (lines 671, 836) and *seyn* (line 1328), but these occur as rhyme words. Present participles are in *-yng*; the one exception is *perand* (line 879), a northern dialectal form. The past participles of strong verbs are inflected with *-yn* or *-n(e)*, though the scribe is not always consistent. The past participles of some historically strong verbs have no ending, such as *found* (line 211), *born* (lines 36, 315, etc.), and *smet* (lines 19, 119), but *take* (lines 707, 1233) occurs with the expected *takyn* (line 1220), *wryt* (line 198) with the more frequent *wrytyn* (lines 52, etc.), and *be* with *ben(e)* (lines 1555, etc.). The verb *have* is sometimes reduced to *a* or *an*, especially when it functions as the first member of a verb phrase. The forms of *to be*, in addition to those mentioned above, include *am*, *art(e)*, *ys*, *ar(e)* or *arn* in the present, *was* and *wer(e)* in the past.

Plural and possessive nouns are normally inflected with *-ys* (*-is* occurs when the preceding letter is *y*). However, the historical plural in *-n* of *eyes*, *eyn* (lines 642, 1026, etc.), is retained, as it was in other dialects until the seventeenth century; but *chyldyr* (lines 48, etc.) has yet to gain the *-n*, which was the plural form for the word in most Southern and South Midlands dialects, and which became the standard. For the personal pronouns, *I* or *Y* is written for the first person subject, *me* for the object, and *my* for the possessive adjective, except when the following word begins with a vowel, in which case the form is *myn*; the plural forms are *we*, *us*, and *owre* or *oure*. Although the historical singular of the second person pronouns — *thow*, *the*, *thy* or *thine* — occur, the poem usually adopts the plural forms, *ye*, *yow*, and *yowre*. This adoption, a polite usage since the thirteenth century, is to be expected in a poem that presents upper-class characters. The third person pronouns are *he*, *hym*, *sche*, *her(e)*, *yt*. In the plural, *thei* or *they* is always the form of the subject. However, the northern *th-* forms are used along with the southern *h-* forms in the oblique cases, so that we find *them* and *hem* as objects, and *ther* or *thayr* and *her(e)* as possessives. Some other notable features of the scribe's spelling include his use of *sqw-* for words beginning with *sw-*; *sch-* for *sh-*; *be* for modern *by*; and his overwhelming preference for *y* instead of *i* or *e*, particularly in inflectional endings.

Certain spelling features indicate that the manuscript had its provenance in East Anglia, specifically, Norfolk.[41] The most prominent idiomatic feature is the use of the initial *qw-* where Modern English uses *wh-*, as in *qwer(e)* (lines 6, 19, etc.), *qwo* (line 1553), *qwat* (lines 63, 65, etc.), *qwyche* (lines 9, 34, etc.), *qwedyr* (lines 1054, etc.), *qwyl* (lines 114, 293, etc.), *qwele* (*wheel*, line 389), and *qwalle* (*whale*, line 578). This *qw-* spelling is an independent development of East Anglia, not related to similar spellings in texts from Scotland and the northern English counties, and it is more prevalent in Norfolk than in Suffolk. A second significant feature of East Anglian scribes is variation in the spelling of *-ght* words with simply *-t*, *th*, or *ht*. The scribe of Garrett 141 is fairly consistent in spelling words like *right* and *might* with *-ght*, but the plural *knytys* appears frequently. Words like *thought* and *daughter* are less consistently spelled than the *right* group, with *-t* occurring about as often as *-ght*. Examples of the *-t* spellings are *browt(e)* (lines 189, etc.), *boute* (line 1863), *wythowt(e)* (lines 440, etc.), *aucte* (line 142), and *wrowt* (lines 700, 1655). Because of the confusion in spelling words ending in a *-t* sound, the scribe has sometimes extended *-ght* to words where it has no etymological basis, including the native English words *wryght* (lines 524, 2171; Modern English *write*, from OE *writan*) and *qwyght* (lines 495, 536, etc. Modern English *white*, from OE *hwit*) and French borrowings *endyght* (from OFr *enditer*) and *ermyght* (lines 1901, etc.; Modern English *hermit*, from OFr. *h'ermite*). Something similar has happened in the spelling of third person singular verbs ending in *-tht*, mentioned above. This spelling, a third hallmark of East Anglian scribes, has been extended sporadically in this text to nouns ending in *-th*: *myrtht* (line 406), *weltht* (line 1134), *trwtht* (line 1151), *ertht* (line 1480), and *detht* (line 1682).

The scribe of *Amoryus and Cleopes* exhibits a number of other secondary dialectal spellings and lexical choices indicative of an East Anglian origin. The spellings of *mend* (lines 1105, etc.) and *kend* (line 1246) and *kendly* (lines 1252, etc.) for Modern English *mind* and *kind*, although not exclusive to eastern texts, when combined with the other features like the *qw-* spelling, further indicates an East Anglian origin. Similarly, the spellings of Modern English *worldly* without the first "l," as in *wordly* (line 379) and *wordely* (line 1911), are unusual variants of a characteristic East Anglian form with "e" as the main vowel: *werdly*. The typical form in the manuscript of the past plural of *to be* is *were*, but two instances of the Scandinavian-influenced form *wore* (lines 1533, 1577) indicate a Norfolk scribe. The scribe's exclusive use of *ony* (lines 156, 179, etc.), as opposed to the standard London forms of the time, *eny* and *any*, further marks the text as

---

[41] For the most complete account of the dialect and orthography of late medieval East Anglia, see Richard H. L. Beadle's unpublished dissertation, *The Medieval Drama of East Anglia: Studies in Dialect, Documentary Records, and Stagecraft*, 2 vols. (York: University of York, 1977), 1: 48–78; see also M. B. Parkes and Richard Beadle, eds., *Poetical Works*, 3:54–55; and Norman Davis, "The Language of the Pastons," *Proceedings of the British Academy*, 40 (1955), 199–44.

eastern and provincial. Finally, the obsolete word *swem*, spelled *sqweme* (lines 1146, 1670; *sqwemful*, lines 843, 1160, 1773, 2046; and *sqwemfuly*, line 1169) in the scribe's normal orthography of *sw-* words, meaning *grief, affliction*, is a dialect word confined in the fifteenth century to East Anglian texts.

The author writes that he composed this poem in the twenty-seventh year of the reign of Henry VI, and there is no reason to doubt this dating. But this manuscript copy of *Amoryus and Cleopes* appears to have been written perhaps as much as a generation after that date. The frequency of plural pronouns *them/hem*, *ther(e)/her(e)* shows a three to one preponderance of the Northern Middle English and incipient standard *th-* forms as opposed to the historical East Midlands forms with *h-*. This northern form did not appear in East Anglia before about 1450, and begins to occur in the Paston letters in 1460. Similarly, the Garrett MS scribe's habit of spelling *-ght* words, those like *right* with *-ght* but those like *thought* with some variation, closely parallels the spelling habits of Sir John Paston II after 1464. Davis suggests that the Pastons' spelling may well have been influenced by their travels and association with the royal court. We may infer that they might exhibit incipient standard English features in advance of a Norfolk scribe. In conclusion, then, it seems likely that the date of the manuscript cannot be much earlier than 1465, and may well have been copied in the 1470s.

The Text of this Edition

This text of this edition of *Amoryus and Cleopes* is based on a microfilm of the manuscript and an examination of the last page of the poem under ultraviolet light. In accordance with the editorial policies of the Middle English Texts Series, scribal abbreviations have been silently expanded and based, where possible, on the scribe's most common, complete spelling of the word. Modern English spellings of Middle English *u/v*, *j/i*, have been adopted, and *gh* and *y* have been substituted for yogh (ȝ). The scribe writes the late form of character thorn, identical to *y*, much more frequently than modern *th-*; this edition has regularized the spelling to the modern form. In addition, the scribe's spelling *Ss-* at the beginning of the poetic line, the only place where he normally employs capital letters, has been reduced to *S*. The scribe also doubles *f* to *ff* in many instances when a capital letter would not be called for: spellings like *ffor*, *ffortune*, *sothffastness*, and *afftyr*, are typical. I have simplified the form according to modern usage. For the sake of clarity, I spell the second person singular pronoun *thee*, where in the MS it is spelled *the*; this alteration does not affect the pronunciation of the word, which in its MS orthography would be understood as having a long vowel. So too in polysyllabic words ending in *-e* (e.g., *cuntré*), I have placed an accent on the *-é* to indicate syllabic value and a long vowel, though not necessarily a stressed syllable. I have followed modern conventions in capitalizing names of persons, deities, and the like. Brackets indicate material not found in the MS which I have inserted for the sake of clarity and syntax. It might be noted that the line numbers in Craig's edition differ from those here, and whereas Craig expanded to *quoth*, I have expanded to *quod*, the more common late medieval term.

Select Bibliography

Manuscript

Princeton University Library, MS Garrett 141, fols. 17b–56b.

Edition

Metham, John. *The Works of John Metham, Including the Romance of Amoryus and Cleopes*. Ed. Hardin Craig. EETS o.s. 132. London: K. Paul, Trench, and Trübner & Co., 1916. Pp. 1–81.

Critical Study

Page, Stephen. "John Metham's *Amoryus and Cleopes*: Intertextuality and Innovation in a Chaucerian Poem." *The Chaucer Review* 33 (1998), 201–08.

Romance Studies

Benson, Larry D. "Courtly Love and Chivalry in the Later Middle Ages." In *Fifteenth Century Studies: Recent Essays*. Ed. Robert F. Yeager. Hamden, CT: Archon Books, 1984. Pp. 237–57.

Gradon, Pamela. "The Romance Mode." In *Form and Style in Early English Literature*. Ed. Pamela Gradon. London: Methuen, 1971. Pp. 212–72.

Mehl, Dieter. *The Middle English Romances of the Thirteenth and Fourteenth Centuries*. New York: Barnes and Noble, 1969.

Pearsall, Derek. "The English Romance in the Fifteenth Century." *Essays and Studies* 29 (1976), 56–83.

Ramsey, Lee C. *Chivalric Romances: Popular Literature in Medieval England.* Bloomington: Indiana University Press, 1983.

Reiss, Edmund. "Romance." In *The Popular Literature of Medieval England.* Tennessee Studies in Literature 28. Ed. Thomas J. Heffernan. Knoxville: Tennessee University Press, 1985. Pp. 108–30.

Stevens, John. *Medieval Romance: Themes and Approaches.* London: Hutchinson, 1973.

Chaucer and the Fifteenth Century

Goodman, Jennifer R. "Chaucer's *Squire's Tale* and the Rise of Chivalry." *Studies in the Age of Chaucer* 5 (1983), 127–36.

Green, Richard Firth. *Poets and Princepleasers: Literature and the English Court in the Late Middle Ages.* Toronto: University of Toronto Press, 1980.

King, Pamela. "Chaucer, Chaucerians and the Theme of Poetry." In *Chaucer and Fifteenth-Century Poetry.* Ed. Julia Boffey and Janet Cowen. London: King's College, Centre for Late Antique and Medieval Studies, 1991. Pp. 1–14.

Lawton, David. "Dullness and the Fifteenth Century." *English Literary History* 54 (1987), 761–99.

Lerer, Seth. *Chaucer and His Readers: Imagining the Author in Late-Medieval England.* Princeton: Princeton University Press, 1993.

Nolan, Barbara. *Chaucer and the Tradition of the Roman Antique.* Cambridge Studies in Medieval Literature, 15. Cambridge: Cambridge University Press, 1992.

Spearing, A. C. *Medieval to Renaissance in English Poetry.* London, New York: Cambridge University Press, 1985. [Especially chs. 2 and 3.]

Strohm, Paul. "Chaucer's Fifteenth-Century Audience and the Narrowing of the 'Chaucer Tradition.'" *Studies in the Age of Chaucer* 4 (1982), 3–32.

Windeatt, Barry. "Chaucer and Fifteenth-Century Romance: *Partonope of Blois*." In *Chaucer Traditions: Studies in Honour of Derek Brewer*. Ed. Ruth Morse and Barry Windeatt. Cambridge: Cambridge University Press, 1990. Pp. 62–80.

————. "Chaucer Traditions." In *Chaucer Traditions: Studies in Honour of Derek Brewer*. Ed. Ruth Morse and Barry Windeatt. Cambridge: Cambridge University Press, 1990. Pp. 1–20.

Literary Culture in Fifteenth-Century East Anglia

Beadle, Richard. "Prolegomena to a Literary Geography of Later Medieval Norfolk." In *Regionalism in Late Medieval Manuscripts and Texts*. Ed. Felicity Riddy. London: D. S. Brewer, 1991. Pp. 89–108.

Bennett, H. S. *The Pastons and Their England: Studies in an Age of Transition*. 2nd ed. Cambridge: Cambridge University Press, 1932.

Gibson, Gail McMurray. *The Theater of Devotion: East Anglian Society in the Late Middle Ages*. Chicago: University of Chicago Press, 1989.

Hughes, Jonathan. "Stephen Scrope and the Circle of Sir John Fastolf: Moral and Intellectual Outlooks." In *Medieval Knighthood IV: Papers from the Fifth Strawberry Hill Conference, 1990*. Ed. Christopher Harper-Bill and Ruth Harvey. Woodbridge, Suffolk: Boydell, 1992. Pp. 109–46.

Kieckhefer, Richard. *Magic in the Middle Ages*. Cambridge: Cambridge University Press, 1990.

Lester, G. A. "The Books of a Fifteenth-Century Gentleman, Sir John Paston." *Neuphilologische Mitteilungen* 88 (1987), 200–17.

Moore, Samuel. "Patrons of Letters in Norfolk and Suffolk, c. 1450." *PMLA* 27 and 28 (1912 and 1913), 188–207 and 79–105.

Amoryus and Cleopes

Thys ys the story of a knyght, howe he dyd many wurthy dedys be the help of a lady, the qwyche taught hym to overcome a mervulus dragon, the qwyche was an hundred fote longe. And this knyght was clepyd Amoryus, and the lady Cleopes. [1]

	The chauns of love and eke the peyn of Amoryus, the knygt,	*What befell in; also*
	For Cleopes sake, and eke how bothe in fere	*together*
	Lovyd and aftyr deyd, my purpos ys to endyght.	*died; compose*
	And now, O goddes, I thee beseche of kunnyng, that Lanyfyca hyght:	*is called*
5	Help me to adornne ther chauns in sqwyche manere	*what befell them in such*
	So that qwere this matere dotht yt reqwyre,	*where; matter; does*
	Bothe ther lovys I may compleyne to loverys dysyre.	
	In May, that modyr ys of monthys glade,	*mother; glad*
	Qwan flourys sprede, the qwyche wythin the rote	*When; which; root*
10	In wyntyr were clos, that than wyth floure and blade,	*closed; then; leaf*
	For Phebus exaltyng, wyth sundry hwys smellyd sote;	*hues; sweet*
	And byrdys amonge the levys grene her myrthys made,	*their gladness*
	Qwan Nero Asy gan to suldwe to the empyre,	*Asia; began; subdue*
	And besegyd the emperoure of Persé, Kyng Camsyre;	*Persia*
15	For qwan this Romaynys gan to subdw	*these Romans; subdue*
	The regyon of Persé and of Medys,	*Persia; Media*
	Camsyr, kyng of that cuntré, hys pepyl to rescwe,	*country*
	Ayens this emperoure in the pleyn of Pansopherys	*Against*
	Toke batel; qwere he was smet to deth at onys,	*where; struck; once*
20	Wyth the ston of an engyne, and hys pepyl put to flyght.	*catapult*
	Thus thise Romaynis became ther lordys wyth fors of fyght.	
	And for fere, the lordys of that regyon	*fear; realm*
	Yeldyn the keys to the emperour of this forsayd cyté,	*Yielded*

---

[1] [**Headnote: be**, by; **qwyche**, who; **qwyche was an**, which was one, **fote**, feet; **clepyd**; called]

Amoryus and Cleopes

	Yevyng hym omage and possessyon	*Giving; homage*
25	Of alle this forseyd regyon of Persé,	
	Besechyng hym undyr trybute for to be;	
	And theruppon ther othe thei toke,	*oath*
	Sqweryng upon the tempyl boke.	*Swearing*

	But for that this contré was gret and populus,	*Because; populous*
30	And feyth in thraldam ys selde seyn, [1]	
	Be sad avysement, the emperour wrought ryght thus:	*By serious*
	He commaundyd to a counsel, in certeyn,	*in truth*
	Alle erlys and barounys that to ther oste dyd perteyn;	*earls; barons; host*
	In qwyche counsel for surenes to reule the cuntré,	*security; rule*
35	They promotyd too lordys to be resydent in the chef cyté,	*two*

	The qwyche lordys were Romaynys born,	*which*
	That aftyr, for prudent port and governauns,	*demeanor*
	Were crounyd kyngys of the remys namyd beforn.	*realms*
	And so this emperour, wyth vyctoryus chauns	*victory's fortune*
40	Returnyd to Rome wyth hys oste and pysauns,	*army; pagans*
	Thyse princys dwellyng in pes and rest	*peace*
	In the chef cyté of Persys, namyd Albynest,	

	Qwere thei despousyd wyvys of the lynage	*married; lineage*
	Of Daryus, sumtyme emperour of that cuntré,	*Darius; formerly*
45	Multyplying the world, as seyth myn autour Fyrage,	
	Qwere he tellyth the ryalté of ther maryage,	
	Remembryng the love and eke the adversyté	*also*
	Of Amoryus and Cleopes, that were the chyldyr dere	*children*
	Of thise lordys, how thei lovyd and dyid in fere.	*died together*

50	And the sempyl wryter besechyth of supportacion	*assistance*
	For the rude endytyng of this story.	*composition*
	But every word ys wrytyn undyr correccion	*subject to correction*
	Of them that laboure in this syens contynwally;	*art; continually*
	For fulle herd yt ys, I knowe yt veryly,	*truly*

---

[1] *And loyalty [of those] in servitude is seldom seen*

55	To plese the pepyl; but the sqwete frute schewyth the gentil tre,	*sweet*
	And the mowth the hert — yt wyl none odyr be.	*heart; other*
	But cause qwy that I this boke endyght	*the reason why*
	Is that noqwere in Latyne ner Englysch I coude yt aspye,	*nowhere*
	But in Grwe Y had yt, wrytyn — lymynyd bryght —	*Greek I; illuminated*
60	Wyth lettyrrys of gold that gay were wrowght to the ye.	*eye*
	That causyd me to mervel that yt so gloryusly	*marvel*
	Was adornyd, and oftyn I enqwyryd of lettyryd clerkys	*literate clerics, scholars*
	Qwat yt myght be that poyntyd was wyth so merwulus werkys.	*furnished*
	But alle thei seyd that yt was, be supposyng,	*in their opinion*
65	Grwe; but qwat yt ment thei nyst ryght noght at alle.	*Greek; knew not*
	And as yt fortunyd, ther come rydyng	
	To Norwyche a Greke, to home I schewyd in specyal	*whom*
	Thys forsayd boke, and he iche word bothe gret and smal	*each; great*
	In Latyne yt expugned; and thus be hys informacion	*translated; by*
70	I had the trwe grownd and very conclusyon.	

Here Endyth the Prolog and Begynnyth the Fyrst Boke

	In Albynest, the chef cyté of the regyon of Parsé,	*Persia*
	Thyse lordys reulyd, the wyche excellent were of fame,	*ruled*
	Be hos prudens the cyteceynys were governyd in pes and equité	*By whose*
	Be longe contynwauns, never founde in blame;	*duration of time*
75	Nout wythstondyng ther charge was, in the emperourys name,	
	Alle maner of trespas to chastyse; but ever wyth ryghfulnes	
	Thei coude alle materys reforme and redres.	*matters*
	And as myn autour doth in Grwe specyfye —	*Greek*
	Tellyng yt for a specyal remeberauns —	*notice*
80	Seytht that thise lordys dwellyd so nyghe,	*Says; near*
	That betwene ther placys ther was no more dystauns	*distance*
	Than that a stonwal made the dysseverauns,	*division*
	The qwyche dyvydyd ther courtys and closys	*enclosed yards*
	And ther delectabyl gardyns, in sesun spryngyng wyth lyliys and rosys.	
85	And be ther namys myne autour doth expres	
	Qwyche was the fadyr of Amoryus and of Cleopes eke;	*also*

33

Amoryus and Cleopes

Seyng of bothe, most had in reputacion of worthynes
Was Palemedon, Amoryus fadyr, the most myghty Greke
Alle the regyon of Tessaly thruowte to seke,   *Thessaly; seek*
90 Hos prudent poyntys of were wer so dyvulgate   *skills; war; well known*
That in the chauncys of Mars he stode makeles laureat,   *fortunes; matchless*

Hos sone, as brevely before I dyd expres,   *Whose son; briefly*
Was Syr Amoryus, of home this story in especyal
Makyth mencion, hos beuté and stature bothe, more and les,
95 Myne autour dothe declare on this wyse in general:
Of mene stature was Amoryus, manful and strong wythalle,   *average; courageous*
Wyth coloure bryght and herys broune, fulle of norture and curtesye;   *nurture*
And be hys wysdam, abyl an hole reme to gye.   *because of; realm to guide*

And in hys governauns so demure and dyscrete was he,   *self-government*
100 That iche creature he coude reverens be norturyd jentylnes [1]
Aftyr ther degré, that of pore and ryche yn the cyté.
The fame of hys manhod and of hys lovlynes   *courage, valor*
Was in ryfe; for as thei seyd alle, he was makeles,   *widespread; matchless*
Hys age consydyrryd, hys byrth and nobyl lynage,
105 Besechyng Venus hym to fortune wyth lygkly maryage.

The fadyr of Cleopes, as seyth this story,   *father*
Was clepyd Dydas, hos wurchyp and fame   *honor*
Was spred ful wyde; so that the cyteceynys for a memory   *citizens; memorial*
Lete make a pyler of bras, therin wrytyn hys name
110 And hys benefetys, moreovyr, hys ymage heldyng a frame,   *accomplishments*
In tokyn that be equité he reulyd the toune,   *fairness; ruled*
And eke that the tempyl was of hys fundacion.   *foundation*

My boke tellyth the cause of this remembrauns,   *memorial*
Seyng that qwyl Palemedon wyth the emperour was in batayle,   *while; battle*
115 Dydas had of the cyté the hole governauns;
And sodenly ther come fro hevyn a thundyr and an hayle,   *from; hail*
That yt overthrw the tempyl of Venus, top over tayle;

---

[1] *That he could treat each person with respect according to their rank because of [his] educated nobility*

And Venus, wyth alle ymagys of gold, sylver, and bras,
Were smet to poudyr, bothe more and las.   *smashed; i.e., all of them*

120 Qwan the case of ther ymages were thus befalle,   *chance event*
The cyteceynis for fere fled to Dydas palyse —   *fear*
Bothe prest and seculerys, women and alle —
For socoure and comfort and to here hys avyse.   *advice*
For this thundyr rof ston wallys and housys of mervulus wyse   *tore down*
125 That the pepyl, dysmayd, ferfully on Dydas gan calle   *dismayed; called*
For los of her godys and savacion of ther lyvys in specyal.   *their gods; salvation*

They compleynyd that ther gref and pensyfhede   *anxiety*
Was for ther tresour, the qwyche ordeynyd was be polycye,
For sundry casys, to helpe the communys in ther nede,   *commoners; need*
130 For reperacion of the tempyl eke, and ther lyberteys to fortyfye,   *liberties*
"The qwyche tresur," quod thei, "undyr this hydus skye,   *they said; hideous*
Kofyr and alle, in the tempyl as yt lay,   *Coffer*
Thus brent into aschys yt ys this day."   *burnt to ashes*

And he ful comfortabylly to them ansqweryd in this maner: *reassuringly*
135 "Frendys, be noght abaschyd for this soden case.
I schal a nwe tempyl reedyfye to owre goddes dere,
And yt as rychely aray as the elde tempyl was.   *old*
And eke as myche tresur as ye lest, more or las,   *wish*
I schal of my fre wyl restore that ye no los schal have.   *so that; loss*
140 Thys ys myne entente, so Jubyter my soule save."   *Jupiter*

For the qwyche, the pepyl on kneys before hym dyd falle,   *Because of that*
And yave to hym preysyng, as thei aucte to do.   *ought*
And for this benefet fulfyl, the pepyl in specyal
Lete make this pyler to Dydas Juno.   *caused to be made; pillar*
145 And lykghly yt ys to be so,   *likely*
Hos doutyr, aftyr myn autour, hyght Cleopes,   *Whose; was named*
And as I wryte, her beuté he doth expres:

As Phebus in bryghtenes alle planetys excedyth in general,   *planets*
Ryght so in beuté Cleopes yche erthly creature   *each; person*
150 Precellyd in fayrenes; that yn the reme in specyal   *Excelled; realm*
The fame of her beuté was spred, and of here stature.   *her*

35

	For so womanly was sche, so benygne to yche creature,	*benign*
	That lusty yong knyghtys gret parte wold make	*opposing sides in a combat*
	To breke huge sperys fersly for Cleopes sake.	*spears*

155 And brevely this proces for to trase   *briefly*
     Qwat that Nature myght werke to beuté in ony creature
     Was wrought in the persone and in the lovely face
     Of this lady, for sche proporciond was in sqwych mesure   *so harmoniously*
     That sche sempt be outeward apparens to pase nature,   *seemed; surpass*
160 Hos beuté thus floryscyng I omyt, as of the douter of Venus,   *daughter*
     Contynwyng here fortunat fate undyr Mars furyus. [1]

     But now of descrypcionnys I sese and forth this proces.   *cease; story*
     As myn autor dothe wryte, ryght so wul I,
     Word for word, save only a lenger progres
165 Yt nedyt in Englysch; for in Latyne he that wrytyth most schortly,   *concisely*
     Most ys comendyd; qwerfore that myn autour endytyth, in more and les,   *writes*
     Compendyusly he pasyth; and so I, in termys fewe,   *proceeds*
     The entent of myne autour I purpos brevely to schewe.   *briefly to show*

     For, as me semyth, yt were a long dygressyon   *it seems to me*
170 To telle howe the nwe tempyl was jonyd of cementaryis,   *new; joined by masons*
     Or to speke of the hythe, or the brede, or of the facion,   *height; form*
     Or the sumpte of goldyn vessellys, as chaudrunnys and fylateryis,   *(see note)*
     Or of Venus chaplet, howe yt was enamylyd wyth grene byris —   *berries*
     To longe yt were to wryte; for myn autour pasyth schortely,
175 And I to prolonge yt were but vanyté and foly.

     In June, the qwyche the nest month ys aftyr May,   *next*
     The yere revolvyd fro the tyme the olde tempyl fyl.   *from; fell*
     The nwe was made and complet be twenty day   *by the twentieth*
     In alle ornamentys that longe to ther sacrifyce be ony skyl,   *by what is fitting*
180 For the qwyche the gentylys alle and eke the commune pepyl   *nobles; commoners*
     Be one asent dyd wryte to Palamedon, of hys devocion,   *of his reverence*
     Besechyng hym to come to ther nwe templys dedycacion.

---

[1] *Continuing [to write about] her fate, governed by fortune, under furious Mars*

And eke the bylle dyd specyfye that yf yt to hys plesauns   *petition; pleasure*

None ofens schul be, thei dysyryd to have a syte   *should; sight*

185 Of Amoryus, besechyng hys hynes noght to take to grevauns   *highness*

That thei bold were on this wyse to wryte,   *manner*

To accepte her feythful entent in hys syte.   *their; sight*

Of odyr thingys the bylle eke dyd specyfy,

The qwyche charge noght here to be browte to memory.   *recalled*

190 But this pepyl a masyngere to the emperour, in goodly wyse,   *messenger; courtesy*

Sent in hast wyth this forsayd bylle;   *haste; epistle*

The qwyche hys masage schewyd wyth ful sad avyse   *serious manner*

Be mowthe, as he was taugh of this pepyl.   *instructed by*

And aftyr delyveryd hys lettyr and held hym stylle

195 Tyl Palamedon had red the ful sentens,   *comprehended the full substance*

The qwyche upon this wyse he told in opyn audyens:

"Lordyis and frendyis," quod he, "owre cyteceynis of Albynest

Have wryt to us that to owre goddes ys fabryfyid   *fabricated*

A nwe tempyl; to the qwych consecracion, at ther reqwest,

200 We muste hye; for in the bylle yt ys specyfyid   *hurry*

That alle ornamentys be alle redy to the solempnyté puryfyid,   *purified*

And noght thei abyde but us and yong Amoryus.

The sentens of this bylle maketh mencion ryght thus."

And qwan he had spokyn, the bariunns that were in his presens   *barons*

205 Alowyd hys sentens and seyd yt was for the best   *accepted his judgment*

To enclyne that tyme to the pepillys sentens: *people's opinion*

"For sythyn," quod thei, "oure lege is now in rest   *since; liege (i.e., Nero)*

Fro Marcyan labourys, he hath of werreyowris the lesse brest.   *warriors; need*

Us thynke best that ye informe hym, as sone as ye may,   *We think; soon*

210 To purvey yow homeward tomorow or the nest day."   *convey yourselves*

And sone a tyme oportune he had found,

Aspyid qwere the emperour was walkyng in a fresch herber,   *garden*

Beforn hym on hys kne he fyl to the ground,

Schewyd hym the entent of hys comyng in benygn maner.   *benign manner*

215 And qwan he had spokyn, the emperour wyth debonayre chere   *disposition*

Sayd to Palemedon, "Do in this matere as ye thinke best.

Ye knowe wele how owre empyre ys now in rest.

	"And for yowre labour in werris that wyth us ye have be,	*wars; been*
	We thanke yow; and we wul, if ony case falle,	*order, if any thing happens*
220	That yowre help in alle godely hast redy be."	
	And qwan he had thus spokyn, hys styward forth he dyd calle,	*steward*
	Comaundyng hym to fecche that ryche purpyl palle,	*robe*
	That hymself had usyd in Mars sacrifyse,	
	The qwyche he yaf Palamedon for hys trw servyse.	*gave; true*

	For the qwyche yift, in parte to make recompens,	*gift*
225	He lovyd hym as prynce, Mars knyght most excellent.	
	And bothe he and Amoryus ful norturely toke ther lycens	*courteously; leave*
	Of the emperour and the courte, and faste thei bement	*intended*
	To hast ther jurney to the forsayd entent;	*hasten*
230	For the qwyche, knytys and odyr gan fast purvey	*others; quickly prepare*
	The nest morow them toward Albynest to convey.	

	An artyfycer nowe were nede to me	*literary artist; necessary*
	That coude a straunge style puryfye;	*refine*
	For my poyntel so rude ys, as ye may opynly se,	*pen*
235	Yt can noght grave, ye may yt wele aspye,	*write (engrave)*
	Be the qwyche my rudenes I mene to endyte this storye.	
	But trwth ys seyd: blynd Bayard of no dowtys doth purvey, [1]	
	Tyl he hath fallyn in the myd wey.	*in the middle of the path*

	Qwerfore fully I me excuse, or I ferther procede,	*Wherefore; myself; before*
240	To yche dyscrete persone most in specyal.	*individual*
	And to the goddes that Fame hyght, now in this nede,	*is called; need*
	I beseche for help — that qwere this boke in chambyr or halle	
	Be herd or red, sche lyst the sylver sqwete pype so smal	*melodious*
	To sounde, that the brasyn trumpe of obloqui,	
245	For my rudenes, mystune noght in no company. [2]	

---

[1] *But [when] truth is spoken, blind Bayard does not take precautions against any dangers*

[2] Lines 243–45: . . . *she might wish the harmonious silver pipe [of fame] so small / To sound, so that the brazen trumpet of oblivion, / Because of my lack of refinement, make no discord before any audience*

And nowe my autour I muste folow in astronomy,
The qwyche dymme ys to onlernyd folk, I trowe verily. [1]

But now I returne to Palamedon, the qwyche lay in rest,
Abydyng sum tokyn qwan Aurora schuld sprynge.   *Awaiting (see note)*

250 And as he lay wakyn, he herd a ruschyng of a chest,
For qwyche noyse he wythowte taryinge
Styrt up to wyte yf ony creature were styryng.   *Sprang up to know*
"Ho goth ther?" quod he; and aftyr stylle he stode for to here   *goes; hear*
Yf ony servaunt had walkyd ther nere.   *near*

255 And to the mortere of wax he yed to aspye the wast, [2]
To wete yf tyme were fore to ryse,   *To know*
To knowe allso how fer the nyght was past.   *far*
And as he the brennyng of the mortere gan devyse,   *burning; examined*
The nyght chauntour, the cok, hys fyrst salme dyd appryse. [3]   *psalm attempted*
260 "A!" thought he, "this sygnyfyith mydnyght.
The cok none ere crwe; yt wul be long or yt be daylyght."   *earlier; before*

Forth than to the wyndow he yed to wyt how the day schuld preve;   *went*
And as he kyste up hys eye to the fyrmament,   *cast*
He aspyid Latona, how sche toke her leve   *the moon*
265 Of Jovys her love, and howe Boetes gan dreve   *drove*
Hys bryght plowgh of sterrys, and eke the systyrrys at ther stent,   *Pleides*
The qwyche be namyd the sterrys sevyn,
How thei gan appere in the myddys of hevyn.

And as he hys chere turnyd to behold Pegasus,   *face*
270 The fyry goddes of the fyrmament gan to schew here face.   *fiery; her*
And qwan he hys lady aspyid, that namyd ys Venus,
Wyth devoute preyyer to beseche her of grace   *prayer*
On kneys doune hym sett, and for this preysyng gan race   *rushed on*

---

[1] *Which is dim to uneducated people, I truly believe*

[2] *And to the bowl of wax with a wick used as a nightlight he went to see how far it had burned (i.e., how much wax it had consumed)* [N.b. OED *mortar* 2 and *waste* ab. 8 a & b.]

[3] *The night cantor, the cock, his first psalm [crowing] attempted (raised up ?)*

	In magnyfying the gloryus chyvalry stellygerat	*exalted to the heavens*
275	In qwemyng of Venus and Mars that than were at debat.	*So as to please; debate*

	"O!" quod he, "Ye inmortal goddyis, alle incorporat,	*said; incorporeal*
	The qwyche be pasyng of nature have trancendyd this mysery	*by surpassing*
	Be fortunat fate, eternally deyfyid and gloryfycat,	*By; glorified*
	That ye the hevyn crystallyne illumyne and puryfye	
280	Of yowre infynyte goodenes, ye yowre wurchypperys deyfye.	*worshipers*
	Be a prerogatyfe synguler, that thei that can yow feytfuly plese, [1]	
	Ye yef them alle that ys to ther hartys ese.	*give; their heart's ease*

	"O, hye Saturne!, reulyng wyth the septyr of prudens,	
	Alle terrenal accionnys cyrcumscryvyst indefycyentlye	
285	Be the progeny deyfyid of thee — havyng decens	
	In fyre, aer, lond, and see [2] — be ther namys them thus to applye:	
	As Jovys, fyry; Juno, aery; Neptunus, wattry; Pluto, erthy;	
	The qwyche, havyng of thise elementys septrat powere,	
	Thy chyldyr were iheryid; be thow and eke thei in fere. [3]	*together*

290	"And eke, O Appollo!, to hos bryght chere my goddys alle	*face*
	Yeve sted; and every lyvyng erthely creature,	*Give way; person*
	Wyth erbe, floure, and frute, thee preyse in general,	
	And eke I thi servaunt, qwyl my lyfe wul endure.	*while; will*
	In my jurny, fyry and noght wattery do thi cure	*journey; duty*
295	To appere, I thee beseche; and I on thee most reverend wyse	
	A blake bole in the yle of Delfos schal to thee sacrifyse.	*bull; isle*

	"And O Mars, cheveteyn of nobyl weryouris,	*chieftain; warriors*
	Wyth Venus and Lucyna, the mone, pesybyl be;	*moon, peaceable*
	For masculyne furyus ayens femenyn schouris	
300	Amonge goddys ys ascryvyd but to crwelté. [4]	

---

[1] *By an exclusive right, [you give to them] that can faithfully please you*

[2] Lines 284–86: *All terrestrial actions [you] constrain unfailingly / By [your] deified progeny, who have descent [from you] / In fire, air, land, and sea*

[3] Lines 288–89: *Your children, who having over these elements unshared power, were praised; may you and also they together be [praised]*

[4] Lines 299–300: *For masculine fury in response to feminine showers / Among the gods is ascribed as cruelty*

And now, howe gloryus and how blyssyd yt ys to se
Yowre deyifyid cherrys, O goddis and goddessys alle.   *faces*
Iheryid ye myght be eternally wyth infynyte memoryalle!   *Praised*

"And O eke ye nobyl deyfyid sygnys! abstracte   *extracted*
305   From erthly mancionnis to the asuryd fyrmamente;   *securely established*
Sum fyx and sum revolvyng to and fro, in maner of the cateracte,
Betwene the poolys — bothe the qwyche namys thus represent   *poles*
The poole Artyk and the poole Antartyk — at the goddys entent
In sundry fygurys, as summe stondyng, summe syttyng,   *some*
310   Sum defendyng, summe lying, summe water poryng.

"And be the hye provydens of yow, goddys colegyat,   *high; collegiate*
Every sygne dysposyd ys be fatal ordynauns   *predetermined*
That yche regnyth a tyme, hys cours kepyng and estate, [1]
Yche, aftyr hys dysposycion, reulyng wyth fortunat chauns   *its nature*
315   Them that born be undyr ther dyverse demenauns —   *rule*
As summe to prosperyté and ese, summe to travel and gret vexsacion,   *travail*
Sum to be leccherus, and sum onstabyl aftyr the sygnys dysposycion.

"Qwerefore, O Alna! wombe of the Sagyttary of sterrys lucent,   *brightly shining*
Myself I deprehend that in thine exorte   *understand*
320   I born was. O blyssyd sygne, fortunat appere to myne entent!   *blessed; plan*
And I thi gloryus fygure of pure gold, to thine apport,   *offering (gift)*
Amonge my goddys schal fyx, and ever to thee resorte
Wyth sacryfyse; and alle sygnys of the fyrmamente, becaus of thee,
Wythin my tempyl in ther lykenes made schal be."

325   And Palamedon thus hys preyur than dyd conclude,
For of sqwetnes of devocion half raveschyd was he,   *sweetness*
Foryetyng hymself; for trwe yt ys that love dothe exclude   *Forgetting*
Bothe hete and cold, and causyth a man foryetful for to be;
For the sterrys so longe he beheld, descryvyng the magesté, *tracing*
330   That the pepyllyng wynde made hys flesch for to quake, *softly blowing*
That he styrt to hys bed and anwe rest began to take.   *hurried; renewed*

---

[1] Lines 312–13: *Every sign is regulated by an invariable ordinance / So that each [god, i.e., planet]*
reigns for a time [in its mansion], keeping its course and its exalted rank

Nowt longe tyme he had loyn in the golden slepe — *lain*

That fro undyr the erthe phyry Phebus — *from; the fiery sun*

Wyth hys glymyrryng bemys into the chambyr gan lepe,

335 That yn hys bryghtnes he woke Amoryus,

And he in hast styrt up and hys fadyr dyd clepe, — *haste; called*

Seyng that yche man redy was to ryde, — *Saying*

Chafyng ther hors up and doune be the court syde. [1]

And be that tyme he redy was to take hys palfrey, — *horse*

340 Lusty, fresch knyghtys of howsold redy were

To convey hym forth in hys jurney.

And qwan he the entent perseyvyd of hys frendys dere,

Of ther lovyng entente he thankyd hem in benyng manere, — *them; kindly*

Seying as herttyly, "I thanke yow in every degré

345 As yf ye me conveyid home to owre cyté."

But alle hys speche stod for noght, for certenly, thei seyd,

They had sundry erendys into hys cuntré — *country*

And eke dyverse messagys upon hem were leyd; — *laid*

Also ther dysyre was to se the nwe tempyl and the cyté. — *city*

350 And qwan Palamedon sey yt wold none odyr be

But forth thei wold, [2] he thankyd them hertyly,

And toke hys palfray and forth rod myryly. — *rode*

And qwan thei pasyd had the cyté but mylys thre, — *miles*

A losty yonge knyght gan preke hys palfray — *spurred*

355 Toward Amorius. "Qwat sorow eylys thee now," quod he, — *ails*

"That thow thus sobyrly rydyst alle this day? — *seriously*

Be myne hed," quod he, "I trowe that thow hast lost thi pray — *believe; have*

Of summe jentyl woman that dwellyth wyth the empres.

Yt ys nowe thi mornyng, as I gesse. — *mourning; guess*

360 "But wotys thow qwat me thynkyth best? — *do you know what*

Lern this lessun, if thow be wyse of me: — *will learn from me*

Lete no fayre loke reve thee of thi rest; — *fair look rob*

---

[1] *Warming their horses by walking them up and down in the courtyard*

[2] Lines 350–51: *And when Palamedon saw they would have it no other way / But that they would go forth [with him and Amoryus]*

But them that thow knowyst hertyly love thee,

Love them ayen qwyder yt be he or sche.   *in return whether*

365 And ever beware of fayre speche, fore many be ontrwe;   *untrue*

For trost in ontrwe hath made many a man to rwe.   *trust; rue*

"But nowe let alle this musyng matere pase,   *matter to ponder pass*

And be avysyd of perell ayens anodyr tyme."   *again another*

"Ye, brodyr," quod Amoryus, "I trowe that ye have trodyn the trace

370 Of lovys daunce, for of the kalendys ye muse the prime; [1]

For he that hyest on that leddere dothe clyme,   *ladder*

Deppest into wo fallyth qwan he hat lost hys pray.

But trost me veryly, lovyd I so no creature into this day."   *trust me truly*

"Wele," quod this yonge knygt, "this matere longyth to sadnes.   *belongs*

375 But lete yt pase, and syng now sum songe for this sesunne."   *suitable for*

"I graunt," quod Amoryus, "begynne moun youre chauntes;   *must; songs*

But go gete us more felychyp." "Ye, for god!" quod he, "Yt ys resun."

And forth he clepyd foure knytys hos ful devocion

Was set in wordly plesauns, that wyth melydyus chauntyng   *worldly delight, who*

380 Thys song of love wyth lusty voys thei gan to syng: *began*

"Qwan flourys sprede in May, of monthys myryest,

And every byrde hath chosyn hys lovely make,   *mate*

For joye of the sesun amonge the levys grene gan rest

Wyth myry notys syngyng, as I my walkyng gan take

385 Undyr a forest syde. I herd one for hys ladyis sake —

To the goddes of love he gan to compleyn,

And eke to fortune for los of hys lady sovereyn:

"'O, Fortune! Alas! qwy arte thow to me onkend?   *why; cruel*

Qwy chongyddyst thow thi qwele causeles?   *Why change; wheel*

390 Qwy art thow myne enmye and noght my frend,   *enemy*

And I ever thi servant in al maner of lovlynes?

"'But nowe of my lyfe, my comfort, and my afyauns   *confidence (faith)*

Thowe hast me beraft; that causyth me thus to compleyn.   *have bereft me*

---

[1] Lines 369–70: *"Yes brother," said Amoryus, "I believe that you have followed the steps / Of love's dance, for on the first day of the month you meditate all morning*

O bryghter than Phebus! O lyly! O growned of plesauns!   *delight*
395   O rose of beauté! O most goodely, sumtyme my lady sovereyn!

'"But, O, allas! that thru summe enmye or sum suspycyus conjecte,   *conjecture*
I throwyn am asyde and owte of my ladiis grace.
Sumtyme in faver but now fro alle creaturys abjecte
As oftyn sqwownyng as I remembyr her bryght face.   *swooning*
400   But now, adwe for ever, for my ful felycyté
Is among thise grene levys for to be.'"

Thys was the dyte of ther fresch songe and the sentens   *verse; contents*
That thise yonge knytys dyd syng in the jurney,
In specyal for feinere love and presnes   *more refined*
405   Of Amoryus; and thus wyth myry songys and talys day be day,
They schortyd the tyme wyth myrtht and wyth play.   *passed*
And in alle ther myrthys Palamedon rode forth stylly,
Thynkyng alle but vanyté and foly.

But now I leve thise fresch galauntys syngyng in ther lay   *gallants*
410   Wyth mornyng joye, in sqwetnes of songe compleynyng
The absens of ther ladyis soveren in the sesun of May,
To returne to the cyteceynys, the qwych herd of ther comyng,
Nwe clad in a sute wyth ful solen aray,   *solemn*
On horsbak wyth Dydas rydyn owte of the cyté,
415   Abydyng in a pleyn the dystauns of mylys thre,

Tyl of ther spye thei had sum tokynnyng.   *scout; sign*
And at hye none thayr masynger come rydyng apase,   *high noon; quickly*
Enformyng Dydas how that thei come fast by.
Ther comyth myche pepyl, thei occupy myche spase,
420   And than Dydas commaundyd yche man hys dystauns
To kepe fro odyr, and fast than he gan purvey   *prepared*
To mete wyth hym in alle godely hast on the wey.   *(i.e., Palamedon)*

And Dydas ful norturely wyth hys company
Hym welcomyd as to hys oune cuntré,   *own country*
425   And eke the emperourys knyghtys, by and by,
Conveyng them forth into ther cyté,
Qwere thei receyvyd were as thei aucte to be,   *ought*

Of hys lady and odyr of the toune,   *others; town*
Ful solemply conveyid home to hys mancioun.   *solemnly*

430   The nest day folwyng, Dydas and odyr sundry
Of the cyté come to Palamedon and hym prayd   *came*
To asyngne a day qwan the tempyl most convenyently
Myght be dedycat. "Loke ye," quod Palamedon, "I held me payd,   *I am pleased*
Save I wul se beforn howe yt ys nwe arayd;   *before then; newly*
435   For yf ony thing schul lak that schuld the tempyl adorne,
I wold have konnyng thereof beforn."   *knowledge*

And forthwyth he dyd clepe the emperour[ys] knyghtys,
"Wul ye," quod he, "se the nwe tempyl aboughte?"   *about*
"Ye, syre," quod they, "we come hydyr to se nwe sytys."   *hither; sights*
440   And forth thei yede and fast beheld yt wythin and wythowte.[1]   *went*
Ther was castyng of perellys and mevyng of many a dowghte,
But at the last this was Palamedonnys sentens,
Among them alle in opyn audyens:

"Trwly, brodyr Dydas," quod he, "this tempyl ys feyre.   *fair*
445   Venus do yow mede; and I purpose in specyal   *reward*
For a remeberauns of owre goddys alle a spere to repeyre   *sphere to provide*
Of pure gold, to the symylytude as a bal,
Havyng therin the goddys mevyng natural   *moving*
And yche sygnys exort; and be mevyng yt schal represent   *rising*
450   The cours of alle planetys of the fyrmament."

And qwan he had thus spokyn, "Qwere ys," quod he, "Venus secretary,
The qwyche in craftys mekanyk hath experyens,   *manual labor*
As of dyvynacionnys, enchauntements, and of sorcery,
And oftyn in ars magyk hath wrowgt in my presens?"   *arts*
455   But of hys wordys or he had spokyn the full sentens,   *before*
Amonge hem was this forsayd prest of Venus,
For he knwe alle beforn be hys spyryt namyd Incobisus.   *by means of*

---

[1] *There was calculation of perils [by astrology] and removing of many a doubt*

And qwan Palamedon had rehersyd this matere before,   *repeated*
"Syre," quod this secretary, "the labour ys cumbrus and grete.
460 But yf I have stuf to performe yt, in lesse and more
For my bysynes, I purpose noght to lete,   *stop*
So that this day ye wul the gold me gete,   *[if] you will get me gold*
Feythfully, I dar promyse that be this day sevynyght, *by a week from today*
Iche image and cerkyl redy schal be dyght."   *Each; made*

465 "As for that," quod Palamedon, "schal be made no tarying."
And he to hys styward anone yaf this commaundmente, *immediately gave*
As mych gold as he wold ax thidyr for to bryng   *ask*
And eke ryche stonys aftyr the secretaryis entent.   *desire*
"Anone," quod he "thei were delyveryd qwyl I am present." *while*
470 And as he commaundyd, ryght so the styward dyd indede,
Preyng this nygromancyer hym in hys werk to spede. *necromancer*

And ther Palamedon in opyn audyens
Them of the cyté chargyd redy for to be,
On ther legauns and promysyd obedyens,   *feudal obligation*
475 Alle present and absent that longe to the cyté,   *belong*
Wythowte resonabyl cause or gret specyalté,
Aftyr eght dayis, be the custummys olde,
The dedycacion of Venus and the tempyl to hold.

And than owte of the tempyl he yede and the knytys also,
480 Home to hys palyce to theyr refeccion,   *refreshment*
Qwere I hem leve carpyng of the tempyl to and fro, *leave them talking*
To returne to the secratary; the qwyche be conjuracion
Of spyrytys enchauntyth myghtyly be dyvynacion,
Wyth spryngys of cydyr, qwyk colys, and encens, *cedar, hot coals, and incense*
485 Introducyng the spyrytys into hys cyrcumferens.   *circle*

And sone an huge pytte he gan make besyde,   *soon; pit*
Qwere he the gold, sylver, and precyus stonys
Thrw in togydyr and aftyr gan abyde   *Threw*
Tyl he had gadyrryd a multytyde of mennys bonys   *men's bones*
490 And thrwe hem into the pytte all at onys;
For as clerkys wryte, the damnyd spyrytys have delectacion *clerics*
Amonge tresur and ded mennys bonys to make ther mancion. *dwelling place*

46

And redy anone he dyght hys sacrifyse,   *prepared*
Abydyng the oure of hys operacion.   *hour; magical process*
495   Arayd in qwyght, hys cerkyl gan dyvyse,   *Dressed; white; circle*
Wyth carectyrs and fygurys as longe to the dysposycion   *belong*
Of tho spyrytys that have that power in ther jurysdyccion.
And at hye mydnyght he entryd hys cumpas,   *high; circle*
Wyth hys boke and sacrifyse conjuryng apase.   *apace*

500   And wythin schort tyme be excellent craft,
He had introducyd into this forsayd pytt
Sevyn hundred thousand spyrytys or he laft,   *before he left*
And fast ther bond them that thei myght noght flytt,   *bound; depart*
Thow thei had yt sqworn; ther them he schytt   *confined (shut)*
505   And made tho spyrytys so mervulusly werk in fere   *together*
That wythin thre ourys complet was the spere.   *hours; sphere*

And now for to declare the werkyng of this spere,
And eke to name the cerkyllys, fygurys, and sygnys,
The multytude of sterrys — namyd in pannymys manere   *pagan's custom*
510   Goddys of the fyrmamente — and eke the mervulus mevyngys   *movements*
Of the planetys, causyng in thayr regne sundry thyngys   *reign*
In werkyng of nature; alle this this spere dyd represent,
As in frosty nyghtys ye may behold in the fyrmament.

In the este ende of this tempyl this spere apperyd aloft
515   Fyve cubytys fro the ground alwey mevyng   *cubits; moving*
Noudyr hangyng ner undyrborn of herd ner of soft   *Neither; nor*
But alone in the eyar to every mannys eye apperyng   *air*
So mervulus a melody yt causyd to folkys heryng
That half thei raveschyd were be the sqwete armony   *sweet harmony*
520   Of the swyft glydyng of thise cerkyllys by and by.   *circles (i.e., spheres)*

And in the over cerkyl includyng alle this huge werk,
Aftyr astrologerys descripcion, Applanos hyght;
The qwyche undyr, hevyn empure, and as Haly the gret clerk   *scholar*
Doth specyfy qwere he of constellacionys doth wryght,
525   Ys nest; and so vysuually to yche mannys syte,   *next; each; sight*
Abovyn this spere enchauntyd, apperryd over, more and les,
As lyqwyde gold brennyng in a furnes.

But the secunde cerkyl, ther ys no lyvyng creature
That myght yt behold but gretly he schuld wondyr
530 Of the operacion and ryches of that mervulus fygure.
For in that the fyx sterrys were and sygnys mevyng asundyr,   *moving individually*
Sum uprysyng, and sum dessendyng, and sum cerkuly mevyng undyr,   *circularly*
The qwyche multytude, in fere, aftyr paynymys opynyon,   *altogether; belief*
Was clepyd the Colege of Goddys, aftyr poyyetys denominacion. [1]

535 And in the fyrst fyx sygne, the doutyr of Lycaon,   *daughter*
Clad in sterrys of gold, cumpasyng tweyn berys qwyght,   *two white bears*
Wyth a saphyryne serpent stedfastly stondyng in one,   *sapphire blue*
The qwyche the north pole ys clepyd, or Artos bryght,   *north polar star*
Nest home Artophylax stondyng redy for to fyght,   *Next to whom*
540 In the defens of Arcton, clad in a palle smaragdyne,   *mantel green*
Adornyd wyth sterrys of gold, to the centyr hys face dyd declyne;

Upon hos schuldyr the garlond of Adryagne
Aperyd in the symylytude as a ryche topas;   *yellow*
Nest home stode Kyng Hercules that alle Asy wanne,   *Asia won*
545 The skyn of a lyon in ryght arme dyd enbras   *embrace*
Wyth a gleyve of gold dyvydyng the cerkyl or cumpas   *spear*
Of somer; closyd in sterrys flamyng nynetene;
The qwyche in hys exorte of astronomerys hyghly myght be sene. [2]

And be Hercules, the harp musycal of Orphé
550 Was joynyd to the pole of the qwych, as poyetys feyne,
Orphe wyth the sqwete melody from Plutoys fyry see,   *realm*
As fro helle, hys wyfe he harpyd ayeyne.   *from; in the opposite direction*
And undyr this harpe the sqwan that to Jovys dyd perteyne
Was plumyd wyth oryent margaryts; and taward the lesse bere   *pearls; bear*
555 Thyse goddys and goddessys conjoynyd were.

Cephe and Casyep, fayre Andrometé, and semly Persé,
The kyng of Cryse, and nakyd Opylenk involvyd wyth a serpent
Wyth the goldyn arow of Hercules that the egyl dyd sle,

---

[1] *Was called the College of the Gods, in imitation of the poets' name [for it]*
[2] *Which at it rising above the eastern horizon might be seen above by star gazers*

The egyl flying by, and the dolphyn that in the spere ys resydent,   *sphere*
560   And wyngyd Pegasus that made in Boyse the welle oryent,   *Boeotia*
Wyth the triangyl, qwyche imagys were made in her fygurys
Off sundry precyus stonys as of carbunkyllys, dyamaunts, and saphyrys.   *rubies*

But for that this matere ys obscure and to onletteryd noght delectabyl,
I pase schortly; but sythyn I have begunne to descrive the spere,   *since*
565   Brevely I schal conclude, omyttyng colourys as of sylver and sabyl,   *Briefly*
Asure, gold, goulys, and verd; the ennamyllyngys in sundry manere   *red; green*
Of the vestyture of goddys as thei wrowght were in fere   *together*
Be enchauntement; and now the resydu up to descrive,
I pray yow of pacyens; I schal ado belyve.   *do [it] quickly*

570   And nest thise foresayd, Phebus twelve dwellyng placys
Sundryly apperyd, the qwyche be clepyd in commune langage   *common*
The twelve syngnys of the yere, kepyng there pacys   *year; orderly progression*
In this forsayd spere, closyd in oryent sterrys as in a cage,   *enclosed*
As the Ram, the Qwyght Bole, the Tweyn Bredyr of Grekys Lynage,   *White Bull*
575   The Crab, the Lyon, the Vyrgyne, and the Weghtys,
The Scorpyon, the Sagyttary, the Capricorn, the Aqwry, and the Fysschys.

And southe in the spere toward the Octyan   *South Pole*
The Qwalle was, hornyd Padus, the Hare, and Oryon   *Whale*
Wyth the sqwyf Grehound, and fers Prochyon,   *Canis Major; Canis Minor*
580   The schyp of Argus, the Centaure or the monstyr of Chyryon,
The fygure of the Dorys of the Tempyl of Salomon,   *Doors*
Wyth the serpent namyd Ydra, the Pese, and the Crow   *Libra*
And the fysch clepyd Serus; thus thei namyd were a Rome.   *in*

And as I have here rehersyd in the spere nygromantyk,   *magic sphere*
585   Ryght so in the fyrmament the same sygnys be,
As asstrologerys wryte, fygurys to men and bestys lyke   *of; beasts alike*
To the qwyche paynymys dyd sacrifyse for every adversyté,   *To whom pagans*
Settyng them in charys of gold that the pepyl myght them se,   *chariots*
Into the qwyche wykkyd spyrytys entryd the pepyl to ludyfye,   *wicked; deceive*
590   To make them forsake God, and to turment her soulys everlastyngly.   *torment*

And into this owre, the most part of the world ys so made blynd   *hour*
Thorowgh the sotel falsnes of the fend that thei beleve   *subtle; fiend*

To be translat into hevyn qwere thei ther god schuld fynd;   *moved, deified*
For of every sekenes thei wene the idol dyd hem releve;   *sickness; believe; cure*
595   Oftyn he talkyth to hem in ther langage bothe morow and eve;   *day and night*
Qwan thei wyth sacrifyse beseche hym to be mercyfull,
He gladyth them wyth feyre promyssys at the fulle.   *please; fair*

But ayen to returne to the spere and yt to conclude fynally,   *again*
The sevyn planetys to descrive, the qwyche beneth thise odyr   *others*
600   Were resydent in ther tronys, reulyng bodyis of the erth myghtyly,   *thrones*
That for ther excellent power sum ys clepyd the fadyr   *are called father*
To them rehersyd before, and so dere and wurthy   *described above*
To alle ydolatrerys thei be that huge templys to yche of thise syngulere
They edyfye to ofyr in theyr sacrifyse and muse her prayyer.   *contemplate their*

605   And to sum thei sacrifyse for wysdam, as to Saturne,
The qwyche in the sevynt spere hath hys domyny;   *dominion*
To sum for prospperyté and wurchyp, as to Jubyter that makyth returne
In the syxt cerkyl or trone; and to Mars for vyctory
Of her adversaryis that the fyfte trone reulyth myghtyly;
610   And to Phebus for ansqwere of aventurys how thei schul falle   *turn out*
In tyme foluyng, the qwyche the fourth spere reulyth celestyal.

And eke to beuteuus Venus, that femenyn ys of nature,
Lusty fresch galauntys to have ther lykyng dysyre
To her beseche for help qwan thei endure
615   Ony infortune or qwan thei brenne in lovys fyre;   *Any misfortune; burn*
The qwyche goddes reulyth the empyre
Of the thryd trone, to home Dydas for pure devocion   *third throne; whom*
Bylyd the tempyl qwere the spere had the mocion.

And to Mercurry, thei that marchaundyse ocupy   *take up merchandizing*
620   As to god of fortune, thei beseche for prosperus aventure;
The qwyche the secunde trone possedyth; and nest us by,
In the fyrst trone, resedyth the goddes of Dyane that the nyght obscure   *resides*
Temperyth wyth her bryght chere that femenyne ys of nature;   *face*
The qwyche thise paynymys clepe goddes of the see,   *call*
625   Preyng her wyth sacrifyse for the seeys tranquillyté.   *sea's*

And thus I ende this rude descrypcion
Of goddys and the spere to speke of the secretary
That had a fynauns and a fulle conclusyon   *ending*
Of this mervulus spere be the spyrytys aery;
630   That fast than homeward gan hym hye   *hurry*
Speryd the tempyl dorys and to hys chambyr yede,   *Closed securely; went*
Qwere I hym leve slepe yf he can, for he hath nede.   *need*

Fowre days aftyr that made was this werke,
Thys secretary had schewyd alle the spere
635   Upon a nyght to Palemedon, qwan the wedyr was derke,   *weather; dark*
Axing hym yf ony he wold have made in privy maner,   *Asking; secret*
Besyde that, to the reverens of theyr goddes dere.
"Qwat?" quod Palamedon, "ye have made be myne estymacion   *What*
That no lyvyng creature but ye myght to this conclusyon.

640   "O, Venus dere!" quod he, "this werk ys so qweynt and mervulus   *cunning*
That I am astoynyd to behold yt; yt mevyth so fast
Myne eyn dymme of the wundyrful bryghtnes; yt ys so laboryus
That my resun demyth that yt myght noght ever last,   *judges*
For be my wytt I have concludyd and caste   *predicted*
645   That yf yche cerkyl were as thyk as a mylle post,   *even if; mill*
The scharp mevyng schul sone cause yt to be lost."

"Be lost!" quod the secretary, "nay, nay," quod [he], "that schal never be
Qwyl the world enduryth; trost that veryly   *trust that truly*
Qwat wene ye? that the cerkyllys were of that tresur that ye   *were [made] of*
650   To me delyveryd? Nay, thynke yt nowt; that ys but a fantesy!
For one cerkyl takyth more matere than yowre tresur drw holy.   *wholly*
But for a matere of counsel," quod this secretary, "in specyal,
I browt yow now hydyr; I schal noght gab at alle.   *hither; chatter foolishly*

"Qwan complet was the spere as yt ys this owre,   *hour*
655   Sore I dysyryd to knowe how longe yt schuld endure.   *Sorely (Intensely)*
And upon a nyght thys weke in my towre,
I sacrifysyd to Venus, prayng her to do her cure,   *duty*
To schewe me be revelacion, to make me sure
Yf yt schuld sone be destroyd, or late, or never,
660   Or, yf the tempyl overtrw, yf the cerkyllys schuld dyssever.   *overthrown; break*

51

"And as I lay, I fyl wondyrfully aslepe   *fell*
And sodenly in a dreme I was, and that a mervulus.
Me thowt I sey Venus alle mornyng as thow sche schuld wepe,   *mourning; though*
Punchyng me wyth her fote to me seyd rygt thus,
665   'Alas!' quod sche, 'we goddessys may say, for sone to us
Is schape an uttyr exile; for here qwere we were wunt to abyde,   *made; wont*
A crucyfyid man schal take possessyon and us put asyde.

"'And were noght,' quod sche, 'that this hevy case schuld falle,   *grave; happen*
The spere schuld ever endure, veryly;
670   But sythyn thus yt schal be, the same nyght breke yt schal   *since*
That we arn drouyn hens; and thus, alas, everlastyngly   *are driven hence*
Owre wurchyp, owre power, and owre memory   *remembrance*
Owte of this cuntré that crucyfyid man shal fleme.   *cause to flee*
Beleve this veryly; loke that never odyrwyse yow esteme.'   *suppose*

675   "No more sche sayd, but ayen sche yede fro thens sche come,
Wryngyny her handys, sodenly vanyschyd awey.
And I wyth that woke and fast yede home
To my rest; and in my bed as I lay,
Sche eft apperyd to me, and on the same wyse dyd say   *again*
680   As sche dyd before; and this ys cause," quod he, "that I
In specyal sent for yow thus hastyly."

"Trwlé," quod Palamedon, "this I wondyr; but yef no credens   *Truly; give*
That yt schal falle, for we were mad owre god to forsake
And to a crucyfyid man to do ony reverens.
685   For that day that I a damnyd man to my god schal take,   *condemned*
Loke that hevyn schal falle and Venus anwe schal make.   *anew*
But loke for rumour of the pepyl that yow yt counsel kepe. [1]
Telle now no more, for I go home to slepe."

Erly in the morw Phebus, wyth hys golden chare,   *chariot*
690   Hys cors toke to the cerkyl that Cherycos men calle,
Spredyng hys fyry bemys on hyllys and desertys bare.

---

[1] *But because of the uproar [the report of this vision might cause] among the people, keep it to yourself*

52

On the heght day lymyt, qwan the dedycacion schul falle [1]
Of this tempyl, qwere iche man and woman in specyalle
For the fest and the sesun aftyr ther costummys olde,   *feast; appointed time*
695 In her best aray, yede to the tempyl this fest to hold;   *clothing; went*

Qwere alle this pepyl gadyrryd, abydyng Palamedon,
Wondryng gretly of the sqwet melody   *harmonious*
That owte of the tempyl come; and sone ther come anone   *immediately*
Thyse lordys and of alle the cyté the ryche and wurthy
700 In glytytyng gounys that wrowt were mervulusly   *gowns*
Of pure gold and stonys that wondyr yt was to se   *gems*
The arayment of lordys in that solempnyté.   *solemn ceremony*

And qwan this secretary aspyid that thei come nye,   *near*
He lete opyn the dorys, commaundyng the prestys alle
705 Them to aray in there slavennys in hye,   *robes*
That no lettyng schuld be, qwat case sumever falle,   *delay*
"But as sone as Palamedon hath take hys stalle,
Owre servyse we may begynne and owre observauns,   *ritual worship*
For to spede the tyme to the peppyl ys most pleasauns."

710 And wyth that, thise lordys entryd into the tempyl —
And eke the comunnys, thei that sunnest myght.   *commoners; soonest*
But sodenly abaschyd the countenauns of the pepyl   *behavior*
In the beheldyng the wondyr fygure of the spere bryght,   *wondrous*
Makyng sqwyche a melody and flamyng wyth sqwych a lyght   *such*
715 That the pepyl dysmayd as schepe in a thundyr   *sheep; thunderstorm*
Ryght so thei stode and on the spere gan wondyr.

And qwan the pepyl had longe yt behold, the secretary
Commaundyd sylens and to sese of ther jangyllyng,   *cease*
And anone began the holy observans and mystery   *rite*
720 Aftyr paynymmys gyse: thei gan meryly syng,   *custom*
Than yche man drwe hym to prayere wythowte more lettyng,   *delay*
And aftyr, ther rammys, kyddys, and bolys, thei gan sacrifyse
To Venus aftyr ther ollde abhomynabyl gyse.   *custom*

---

[1] *On the eighth and final day [as stipulated by Palamedon, q.v. lines 477–78], when the dedication should take place*

Now leve I this introducyng matere in specyal

725 To declare the substauns of the story:

Of Amoryus and Cleopes beyng at thise mysteryis alle,

In that tempyl ful lytyl knowyng qwat fortune was them ny

Of lovys chauns; for thow thei were born fast by,

Nowdyr of odyr had very knowlech; for as I before told, *Neither*

730 Amoryus was fostyrryd in the emperourys houshold.

Thys Amoryus in the tempyl yed up and downe, *went*

Conveyd wyth thise fresch yonge knytys, *Accompanied by*

Carpyng of aventure; for lytyl devocion *Talking*

They had in the servyse, but alle ther delytys

735 Was to se the gentylwomen, kastyng to and fro ther sytys; *glances*

For one thei spake, fyllyng the champ, yche to odyr, *talking away, each*

But wyth ther mowth thei musyd one and wyth ther hert anodyr. *heart another*

And as Syre Amoryus talkyd, he kyst hys ye covertly *cast; eye*

To beheld thise ladyis, notyng thayre demenauns *self-governance (demeanor)*

740 And eke ther beuté, hys eye began sodenly

To be set on one, abaschyd in maner of that soden chauns, *because of*

Mervelyng gretly that sche wyth so goodely countenauns

Kyste here eye asyde qwan he her beheld stedfastly,

Revolvyd in hys mende that bothe sche was beuteus and womanly. *mind*

745 But alwey he fyllyd the tale amonge them alle *kept up the conversation*

That no creature coude aspye that he was bysy *So that*

About sqwyche materys; but anone he gan calle

A servaunt, byddyng hym hys prayur rolle to fecche in hye

And ayen turnyd to the knytys, "Ye are cause," quod he, "that I

750 Am behynde of my devocionys." "Devocionys!" quod thei,

"Qwat! pray qwan ye ar elde, and talke now; stylle be yowre fey." *subdued; faith*

But at the last this servant come wyth this rolle,

Delyveryd yt to Amoryus, and he wold no lenger lett. *delay*

"Adwegh," quod he to the knytys, "I must grete daune Appolle *Adieu; don*

755 Wyth thise devocionnys," and on hys kneys doune hym sette,

And that thei schuld here loude, thus Appollo he gret:

"In thi preysyng, O god Appollo, my vowe receyve gracyusly

To my comfort and encrese of thi glory."

54

And up he rose, for done was hys gret devocion.

760 But wyth hys rolle, abrod he welk fro the este to the weste,   *abroad he; walked*
And wyse and ware he was that be no maner of suspycion   *wary*
The starerrys aboute schul perseyve, but deme for the best   *Those who stare*
That he so yede; and nere as he durst ever he yede forby the closet [1]
Qwer Cleopes sat, but ever fere of tungys hym let.   *fear of gossip; deterred*

765 But at the last, nere he gan take hys trace;   *course*
And as godely as he coude, he covertly kyst hys ye   *slyly cast; eye*
Upon this lady, and eft forth gan kepe hys pace   *again*
As he had done before, and sche anone gan yt asspye.
But qwy he so her beheld sche knwe noght veryly,   *truly*
770 Save for because of hys godely chere,   *kindly*
Sche dempt that he her lovyd in frendly maner.   *deemed*

And wyth that, sche gan remembyr hys manhed and fame   *courage*
That in ryfe was, and eke hys amyabyl stature.   *widely known*
"O" quod sche, "this ys Amoryus for certen; this ys the same
775 That so manful ys in bateyl and so lovely to yche creature.   *courageous; person*
O Venus!" quod sche, "deme I noght aryte that this wurthy weryour   *judge*
Schuld cast a love to me that fostryd hath be among most beuteuus
Of alle Rome? for certeyn yt ys noght thus,

"But for sum odyr cause he dothe me behold?"
780 And as sche this gan revolve in her mende to and fro,   *mind*
He come forby at her; bak and forth hys cours gan hold.   *near*
And sche anone gan consydyr hys stature as he gan goo,   *immediately*
Comendyng hys semlynes; and sone the delectabyl woo   *woe*
Of lovys fyre had percyd here hert that her ful cure   *pierced her heart*
785 Was hym to love before yche erthely creature.   *in preference to*

And eft wyth hys rolle he come as he dyd before
In hope that he comfortyd schuld be yf he mygt her behold.
And stedfastly he gan her behold; but ever lenger, the more   *longer*
He went to a be holpyn, the more hys hert gan fold. [2]
790 And as he yede softely, he syghyd; and so sche supposyd qwat he wold.   *desired*

---

[1] *That he so went about; and near as he dared, he always went nearby the enclosure*

[2] *He proceeded to have been cured, the more his heart grew faint*

But ho was than joyful but sche qwan sche herd that syghyng?　　　　*who*

For more plesauns yt was to here than ony erthly thyng!　　　　*delightful; hear*

There was no wytt than to seke, in sothefastnes,

To conclude undyr qwat form thei myght aqweyntyd be.[1]

795　　A thowsand weys thei kyst thayre love to expresse,　　　　*contrived*

But redy womannys wytt ys yn soden casys of necessyté.

And so Cleopes there schewyd to make in love an entré,　　　　*revealed how*

To save her worchyp and that Amoryus schuld have knowyng,　　　　*honor*

Be a fygure, the entent of her inward menyng.　　　　*By a sign; meaning*

800　　There was, as seyth the story, a portrature mervulus

In a boke that Cleopes had to sey on her devocionys,　　　　*with which to say her*

Portrayd wyth gold and verd, the qwyche conseyt representyd thus:　　　　*green*

Ther was an hynde lying as yt had bene on stonys,　　　　*hind; as if*

Holdyng an hert that bordyryd was wyth trw lovys,　　　　*heart*

805　　Beforn qwyche depeyntyd was a knyght knelyng,

Holdyng in one hand an hart, in the odyr [a] ryng.　　　　*heart*

But qwy yt was portrayd, ne fallyth me to telle

But for the conseyt womannys wytt to expres.[2]

Thys lady had caught an ymagynacion of that mervel,　　　　*conceived a scheme*

810　　That in lyke thingys the dome lyke schuld be, sche gan ges,　　　　*opinion; guess*

"And yf he wyse be, my menyng he schal perseyve in more and les."

And as he yede forby, sche held aloft her boke, and bysyly　　　　*near; busily*

Her ymagys beheld, and Amoryus yt gan aspye.

But that he mervelyd that sche wyth so sad chere　　　　*steadfast*

815　　Beheld her boke, and wythin hys hert purposyd fully　　　　*intended*

To wytt qwat yt schuld be be sum maner　　　　*know; by some means*

That sche wyth stedfast chere beheld so bysyly.

And as fortune wold, Venus was born foreby　　　　*near by*

To hos reverens iche man and woman on kneys them set,

820　　And Amoryus doune knelyd be Cleopes closet.　　　　*down*

---

[1] Lines 793–94: *There was no idea then left unexplored, in truth, / To resolve under what means they might become acquainted*

[2] Lines 807–08: *But it does not fall to me to explain why it was portrayed, / But only to [tell of] the ingenious device that expressed [this] woman's plan*

Fyrst, he dyd be norture obeychauns that straungely, [1]
And sche hym rewardyd ayen with wordys soft.
But qwat he seyd or sche, my boke makyth no memory,
Save qwan that Venus was born alofte,

825   Hys eye on Cleopes boke he kyst ful ofte,   *often*
And sche a-purpose made wyth her fynger demonstracion
Askauns, "Constrwe now, for of my menyng this ys the entencion."   *As if to say*

And he sone yt perseyvyd and gan revolve to and fro
In hys hert; but no lenger than he dyd abyde,

830   But up he rose and forth in hys walk he gan go,
Revolvyng in hys mende to and fro   *mind*
The portrature that he had sene on every syde,   *thoroughly (on all sides)*
Noght the imagys only, but of the beholdyng
That sche wyth chere and fynger made therto tokenyng.   *as sign*

835   But the servyse endyd; thise knyghtys come in fere   *together*
To Amoryus. "Qwat!" quod thei, "benedicyté! ye arn wunder holy today.
Ye have sayd for alle this weke yowr preyyer!"
"Yee, yee!" quod Amoryus, "sumtyme to sporte and sumtyme to pray
Yt ys expedyent; iwus yit I have thingys to say;   *proper; certainly still*

840   But now, for schortnes of tyme,
Of the resydu I schal abyde tyl tomorgh prime."

Nedys he must depart — but lothe was he —   *Necessarily*
Fro hys lady, and sche wyth sqwemful chere   *sorrowful*
Gan hym behold qwan sche say yt wold none odyr be   *saw*

845   But nede thei must depart. "Farewele," quod sche, "my knyght entere."   *perfect*
And he, "Farewele, my hole plesauns and lady dere."   *whole*
In her hertys thus thei ment, at hos partyng was a privy peyn,   *their*
But at thayr metyng come myrth ayeyn.

Hom iche creature yede aftyr this forsayd solempnyté   *Home; ceremony*

850   To her refeccion, and yche man gan hym hye   *their refreshment (meal)*
To the tornamentys, and most in specyal for to se
The justys that proclamyd were most specyally   *jousts*
At the reqwest of the emperourys knytys, the qwyche bysyly

---

[1] *First, he did by nurture obeisance to that [statue] in pagan fashion*

Than gan them harnes, hying hem to the feld   *Then; put on armor; field*

855   Qwere the knytys of the cuntré abydyn wyth spere and scheld.   *awaited*

And Amoryus nas noght behynde, but yit or he toke hys stede   *was not; before*

A portrayer he clepyd, byddyng hym in alle the hast he may   *painter; haste*

Steyn wyth colourys in a kerchyf of a qwarter brede   *Paint; breadth*

The same conseyt that in Cleopes boke he sey.

860   And this portrayer wythoute delay

Steynyd yt sone, and for he knw Amoryus myght noght abyde,   *knew*

For hast ayens a fyre he dryid the wrong syde.   *dried; underside*

And Amoryus fast this kerchyf gan wynde

Aboute hys ryght arme that men myght yt see,

865   And on hys steede he lepe. "Qwer ys my fadyr? Ys he behyn?"

To hys men he sayd. "He abydyth yow," quod thei, "in the entré."

"And the knytys eke, abyde thei me?"

"Wele," quod he, "here goth therfore." And fast he prekyd to the place,   *rode*

Ther the servaunts telde hym hys fadyr was.   *told*

870   And as he come hys fadyr gan yt asspye   *(i.e., the painted cloth)*

Fro ferre. "Qwat," quod he, "hath he yondyr? Yt ys sum nyseté."   *afar; folly*

As he come nere — "Qwat have ye ther? qwat maner jape or foly?"   *trifle (joke)*

"Fadyr," quod he, "this nyght for a specyal tokyn of vyctory,

Venus apperyd, schewyng this fygure to me,

875   Byddyng me the symylytude to forme, wyth the qwyche wythowte fayl   *copy*

I schuld have vyctory in every tornyament and bateyl."

"God yeve grace," quod he, "yt be so." And forth thei gan ryde   *give*

To this place qwere the knytys abydyn, armyd bryght,

Hovyng on horsbak, perand aboute on every syde   *Waiting; peering*

880   Qwan Amoryus schuld come; and anone ryght   *immediately*

The pepyl gan crye that come to behold that syght,

"Make rome fast, for he comyth, owre lord Palamedon   *room*

Hys sone eke, and the emperourys knytys everychon."   *everyone*

Amoryus and Cleopes

	Sone as the statys had takyn her stagys, [1]	
885	Eke the ladyis of the toune her setys had take,	
	Into the place come rydyng the emperourys knytys, makyng chalengys	
	Ayens alle that wold come party in justys to make	*would take sides*
	That day in the feld, for here soveren ladyis sake.	*field*
	And Amoryus this mowthyd to plese Cleopes,	*announced*
890	For sone he had her asspyid among alle the pres.	*crowd*

	None erthly creature than gladder was than sche	*No; then; than*
	Qwan sche sey this conseyt aboute hys armour.	
	Kastyng alle doughtys asyde, full joyful sche gan be,	*doubts*
	Blyssyng Fortune of that owre	*Blessing; hour*
895	Abydyn; but more glad qwan that he	*Awaited*
	Qwyt hym as a champyon that day in the feld.	*Proved himself*
	"Mars," quod sche, "fro alle adversyteys Amoryus scheld!"	

	And as myn autour dothe wryte, thise justys contunyed	*continued*
	Heght days, qwere to conclude, thise knytys imperyal	*Eight*
900	In tho justys oftyn were onhorsyd	*unhorsed*
	Of knytys of the cuntré, for many a falle	*By; i.e., of Persia*
	They had and eke yowyn; but be lyklenes, the vyctory specyal	*given*
	They of the regyon schuld an had at the conclusyon	*have had*
	Had noght Amoryus hym qwyt as a fers lyon.	*fierce*

	But of alle thise eight dayis, knyght for knyght, non so manly	
905	Hym qwyt as Amoryus, for noght onys he was reysyd	*raised (i.e., unseated)*
	Owte of hys sadyl; and yit yche day he had the vyctory	*yet*
	Of alle that ayens hym rydyn, for of the cuntré the knyghtys nomberyd	
	Sevyn skore that notabyl werryours oftyn had be prevyd,	*been proved*
910	And of the emperourys knytys, wyth alle odyr of the toune,	
	But to and fourty, be ful computacion.	*two*

	Erly on the eght day qwan endyd was the solempnyté	
	Of Venus and the tempyl, Amoryus lete cry among the pepyl alle:	*announced*
	Ayens as many as wold come, he redy schuld be	
915	For hys lady sake to juste ayens yche knyght in general,	

---

[1] *As soon as the estates (people of rank) had taken their [appropriate] seats on the tiered viewing platform*

In hys owne persone, and qwat he were myght yeve hym a falle | *whoever*
Schuld ryghtly hys coursere and trappere possede | *(see note)*
And hys harnes have for hys mede. | *armor; prize*

Thys was the cry of Amoryus in opyn audyens,
920 The qwyche ful sore to her hertys yede that envyus were; | *bitterly; their*
But nowght ther grucchyng myght help, for or he yede thens | *went thence*
In justys a nwe skole he gan hem lere;[1]
For nas ther non so strong but he dyd hym bere | *there was not any*
Owte of hys sadyl, or hors and man yede both to ground,
925 That hys manhod hys adversaryis abaschyd and confound. | *courage*

And casually yt happyd, there come rydyng forby | *by chance; near*
A knyght aventerus that for hys lady sovereyn | *adventurous*
Had foughtyn in kyngys londys sundry. | *lands*
He of thise justys had gret dysdeyn
930 Qwan [he] beheld one overcome so many.
Sone of the pepyl he enqwiryd that stod hym by,
"Qwat ys he yon," quod he, "that thus fersly justyth today
That no knyght hym onhors may?" | *unhorse*

"Syr," quod thei, "yt ys Amoryus, the lordys sunne of this cyté.
935 A more manful man of hys age we trowe lyvyth noght." | *courageous; believe*
"A!" quod this knyght, "ys this Amoryus? Ys yt he?
Wele," quod he, "hys pride this day ful sore schal be bowght."
And wyth owte wordys moo, he rode into the place, | *more; arena*
And to Amoryus thise wordys spake wyth sterne face:

940 "I chaleng thee," quod the knyght, "qwatsumever thow be, | *whoever*
To fyght wyth in the lyst for thi lady sake, | *jousting arena*
At alle poyntys of armys; and yf thou dar mete wyth me, | *skills of fighting*
Yeve an ansqwer, for I none odyr day wul take."
And Amoryus ful norturely sayd, "I," quod he, "for my lady sake | *gallantly*
945 Redy am, but as ye may be resun consydyr,
To fyght on fote I am noght now arayd theraftyr.

---

[1] Lines 921–22: *But their complaining did not help at all, for, before he left that place, / He taught them a new lesson in jousting*

60

"But fyrst wyth scharp sperys one cours let us asay,   *passage; try*
And aftyr I schal chonge myne harnes to yowre entent."   *armor; desire*
"I graunt in feyth," quod this knyght, "I schal never say nay.
950   But ho ys lord," quod he, "of this tornament?"
"My lord, my fadyr," quod Amoryus, "he syttys here present."
"Wyth hym wold I speke," seyd the knyght. And wythowte more,
He browt hym syre Palamedon before;

To home, as knyghthod askyth, he yaf informacion —   *whom; requires; gave*
955   Qwat he was, and qwy he come, and of the chalenge
Made to Amoryus; and qwan he herd hys conclusyon,
Sumqwat asstoynyd, for hym thowt straunge and alenge
Of hys aray for the colourys and qweynt facion.   *weird alien dress*
But at the last, he welcummyd hym goodely,
960   Grauntyng the efecte of hys dysyre fully;

Comaundyd eke to be led to hys palyce,
And wyth alle humanyté to be refreschyd before hys labour.
But the knyght noght wold for crwel hert and malyce,
Seyng, "I dysyre no reward of toune ner towre."
965   "Wele," quod Palamedon, "begynne yowr fyght this same owre
I held me payd." But trwe that proverbe than prevyd so,   *then proved*
That over-hasty man wantyd never woo.   *woe*

But qwy I rehersyd before that Palamedon gan wondyr   *related*
Of this knytys aray, this was cause in specyal: *attire*
970   For a tokyn he yt dyd schew that men schuld knowe asundyr
The feld of tho kyngys armys alle [1]
In hos kyngdams he had foutyn, bothe gret and smal;   *whose; fought*
For of yche regyon he bare the chef coloure in hys harnes   *armor*
To notyfye the manhod of hys scharp jurneys.   *exemplify; fierce*

975   For the kyngdam of Ethyop, hos kyng beryth a lyon rampaund   *(see note)*
Of goulys in a feld of sabyl, this forsayd knyght   *red; black*
Blak sabatouns weryd; and for Arge, hos kyng a lebard passaund   *leopard*
Of sylver in verd bare, he usyd grevys that wyth grene were dyght.   *green bore*

---

[1] Lines 970–71: *As a symbol he exhibited it (his strange dress) so that men should be able to distinguish / The background color (field) of all the coats of arms of the kings*

	And for the regyon of Ynde that in the este hat the syght	*India; east has*
980	That asure and gold gerundy bare, hys one cuschew blwe,	*gyrons; cuisse*
	Hys odyr alle depeyntyd wyth yelwe.	

And for the kyngdam of Arabé, hos governour — *Arabia*
A gryfyn of golde in goulys dyd bere,
Thys knyghtys vambracys in coloure
985   Alle depeyntyd wyth red were.
And for the kyngdam of Lyby the qwyche a toure — *Libya*
Of sylver in asure bare, hys rerebracys
Were depeyntyd wyth blwe, hangyng ful of lacys. — *laces*

And alle hys odyr harnes of bryght stele, — *armor*
990   Wythowte depeyntyng: as hys rerebracys and hys gorget,
Hys basenet, and hys gauntelettys; for he purposyd that cele
To a colouryd hys odyr harnes every dele [1]
Wyth the armys of Perse, and so yt was qwan Amoryus wyth hym met.
He clad hym alle in goulys, as I ges, — *red*
995   Qwan overron wyth blod was alle hys harnes. — *overrun*

But schortly to conclude: Amoryus and this knyght
Her cours begunne on courserys huge and mayn, — *Their; powerful*
And at the fyrst metyng Amoryus this odyr gan smyght — *strike*
Upon hys umbrere that the sperehed left in hys brayn — *umbril (helmet visor)*
1000 And so schet hym over hys hors on the pleynne —
Dede, as he must nedys hos servaunts thus pride doth reward — *Dead*
That for hynes of hert at none odyr hath regard. [2]

Thus endyd were the justys and eke the solempnyté
Of the dedycacion, and the laure of Marcyan vyctory — *laurel of Martian*
1005 Yovyn was to Amoryus; and eke my boke tellyth that qwan he — *Given*
Had slayne this knyght, he rode forby — *near*
Qwere Cleopes sate and odyr ladyis, salutyng them godely, — *sat*

---

[1] Lines 990–92: *Without coloring: his armor for his upper arm, and his throat armor, / His helmet, and his armored gloves; for he intended at that time / To have the rest of his armor entirely colored*

[2] Lines 1000–02: *And so shot (threw violently) over his horse onto the plain — / Dead, as one who Pride's servant must be, / Who for arrogance has regard for no one else*

Seyng, "This juberté have I abydyn for my lady sovereyn,   *jeopardy; endured*
And yit nowdyr of us knowyth odyr, I dar savely seyn."   *neither; safely say*

1010   And thei alle rysyn, thankyng hym norturely   *courteously*
       That he hym so manly dyd quyght,   *acquit himself*
       And most in specyal Cleopes gan hym preyse that he so honourly   *praise*
       Had hym born, besechyng Venus hym to deyfy in hevyn bryght: *deify*
       "For gret pyté yt were that owght but goode schul on yow lyght."   *pity*
1015   And Amoryus hys hed gan enclyne, seyng wyth goodely chere,
       "God do yow mede, madame, for yowre goode prayere."   *reward*

       And sone this tournament brake up, and yche man yed ther wey,   *went*
       Thydyr fro thens he come;[1] and the nest morw be pryme,
       The emperour[ys] knyghtys homeward fast schop ther jurney,   *directed*
1020   Thankyng Palemedon of hys gret chere oftyn tyme,
       And eke of the ryche yiftys, wyth the qwych he hem dyd lyme   *he bound them*
       That to the emperour come sone wyth tydyng of Perse,   *To go soon to; news*
       Qwere I them leve floryschyng in prosperyté.

The Prolog in the Thyrd Boke

       O blynd sky of oncunnyng, onys wythdrawe!   *ignorance; at once*
1025   Agytat of thee, precyus modyr, synderesys   *Shake out; cinders*
       That fro the eyn of the endyter longe, to sothsawe,   *in truth*
       In this boke hath schadwyd the qwyght herys   *darkened; hair*
       Of sapyens; but Aqwilo nyl noght blowe wyth hys sylver terys;   *will not; tears*
       And nevertheles, I must procede to declare Venus observauns.   *rite*
1030   Qwerefore, O Lanyfyca! yit onys help me in this chauns.   *circumstance*

The Begynnyng of the Thyrd Boke

       Aftyr thise forsayd justys and eke the solempnyté,
       The desteny of infortune drwe to the conclusyon;   *ill fortune*
       For wythin Amoryus the sparkyl of love so rootyd gan be   *became*
       That he sekynnyd and pale gan wax, in parte.   *sickened*
1035   But lothe he was to be aspyid, qwerefore be symylacion   *seen; by feigning*

---

[1] *Toward that place he had come from*

Beforn folke, he peynyd hym to bere myry countenauns,   *took pains*
But none erthly myrth myght lesse hys penauns.   *penance (suffering)*

For ever the remembrauns off Cleopes so sore dyd hym inquiete   *disturbed*
That qwan he yede to rest and began to slepe,
1040 He dremyd he sey her, or ellys that he wyth here schuld mete —   *saw*
And wyth that abrayd owte of hys slepe and wepe   *woke suddenly; wept*
As yf he had lost hys pray; and aftyr toke hym a cold or an hete   *chill; fever*
Of lovys fevyr that nowdyr mete, drynke, ner play   *neither*
Myght ony maner hys pensyfhed wythdrawe awey.   *in any way; pensiveness*

1045 And undyr the lyke forme, Cleopes gan remembyr   *in a similar manner*
A thosand tymys Amoryus qwan sche was alone,   *times*
Syghyng oftyn for hys sake; for ever lovys fevyr
Here so scharply held that oft sche made her mone   *complaint*
For hys absens, and be herself bothe syghe and grone,   *sigh; groan*
1050 Seyng oftyn, "O Amoryus, alas that I ever sey thee!   *Saying; saw*
Thy goodelynes my deth sone schal be."

Thus, day be day, her grevauns thei dyd compleyn   *pain*
Alone, but morwgh and evyn specyally;   *morning; evening*
For than theyr use yt was, qwedyr yt dyd blowe or reyne,   *habit*
1055 Pryvyly to stele owte that no man schuld them aspye   *Secretly*
Into the orteyerdys that to thayr fadyrrys placys dyd perteyne,   *orchards; fathers'*
And ther her mone yche of odyr wold make pitusly
Undyr a walle that dysseveryd bothe placys covertly.   *separated*

Of this walle I spake in the fyrst boke,   *spoke*
1060 That qwan the tempyl of Venus dyd falle
Wyth the erthqwave, in the myddys asundyr yt schoke,   *earthquake*
That yn at a crany a man myght loke —   *So that*
Save that yt overschadwyd was over alle
Wyth yvy and bowys, that thow a man had gone forby,   *ivy; boughs; though*
1065 For thyknes of levys, he myght noght yt asspye.   *Because of*

So yt befyl on a mornyng qwan Phebus schone bryght,
Cleopes, as sche had done before, sche toke her wey
Into this ortyerd qwan aslepe was iche wyght   *orchard; each person*
Of here fadyrrys howsold; and as sche gan pray   *household*

64

1070	To Venus for help, sodenly a glymyrryng lyght	
	Of the sunne yn the levys on her face gan glyde	*glided*
	That yt her astoynyd and made her abyde.	*So that; astonished*
	"Benedycyté!" quod sche, "fro qwens comyth this lyght?"	*Bless me!*
	And fast the walle sche beheld; but long yt was	*diligently*
1075	Or sche yt asspyid, thow sche applyid alle her myght,	*though*
	That yn the buschys and brerys sche gan trace,	*briars*
	Wenyng that the goddes of Venus bryght	*Thinking*
	In sum yvy tre had apperyd for sum mystery	
	That causyd her the faster thidir to hye.	*hasten*
1080	But at the last, wyth gret labour and bysynes,	
	Sche perseyvyd the crany, and than ful bysyly	
	Sche gan in loke, but the bowys and thykke gres	*grass*
	So full on the odyr halve grwe that thru sche say noght veryly.	*clearly*
	But wele the schadow of one sche gan asspye	*well*
1085	Oftyn wandryng to and fro, mornyng and syghyng,	
	And aftyr, wyth pytous voyse, hys grevauns compleynyng.	
	And more and more sche gan lyst to wyt qwat he sayd	*listen to know*
	And wyth the wynde sche herd a compleynt	
	That one of her made as on the ground hym layde [1]	
1090	Seyng, "O Venus dere! how I am now feynt	
	For Cleopes sake!" The qwyche wordys causyd her to abrayd	*spring*
	Thorw the buschys; and to wyt be hys voys ho yt was,	*through*
	Sche thrwe over the bottum of a brokyn glas.	*glass vessel (mirror?)*
	And he therwyth astoynyd, "Ho strowyth therin thus homely?	*strews; rudely*
1095	Be Venus he ys noght taught, qwatsumever he be!"	*whoever*
	And Cleopes hys voyse knw in hye,	*immediately*
	Ansqweryd, "Mercy, dere hert, Amoryus!" quod ssche.	
	"Ho ys that? Cleopes?" quod he, "ys yt ye?"	
	"Ye, for serteyn," sche sayd, "and none but I lone.	*alone*
1100	I mervyllyd ho so ther nowe made hys mone."	

---

[1] *That someone made about her as he lay on the ground*

"Alas!" quod Amoryus, "myne hert wul breke a too   *in two*
But yf I may speke wyth yowe or ye hens wend.   *Unless; go*
Thys wal ys so thyk and so hye, bothe too,
That I may noght. Alas! how schal I doo?"
1105 "Fere yow noght," quod sche, "nowdyr troubyl yowr mend, *nor; mind*
But come to the ryvyng of this same walle,   *fissure (hole)*
For here no man schal asspye yow at alle."

"The ryvyng?" quod he, "qwere ys that?" And forth thru thyk and thyn
He gan lepe that nowdyr nettyl busche ner thorn
1110 Myght hym let tyl he was entryd in.   *impede*
And qwan he had founde yt, he blyssyd that he was born *rejoiced*
Of that owre abydyn; and at ther fyrst beholdyng   *hour awaited*
Bothe to, thei fyl on owdyr syde on sqwounyng. *Each other; swooning*

And aftyr, thei rose and yche to odyr gan compleyn
1115 Wyth pytus voys her hertys grevauns.   *piteous*
And Prince Amoryus thus fyrst gan to seyn,
"Myne hole hert, my lyfe, and my lady sovereyn,
To serve yow before alle odyr wythowte repentauns   *regret*
Is my hole entent, and ever to do yowre hertys plesauns
1120 Every owre, bothe day [and] nyght,
To serve yow before alle odyr, my trwth I plyght. *trouth (faithfulness); I pledge*

"And ther ye say onys yea, schal I never say nay,   *If; once; yes*
But ever do my bysynes qwyl my lyfe wul endure *diligently labor while*
To be yowre trwe servant; qwat schul I more say?"
1125 "Truly," quod Cleopes, "and I before every creature *in preference to*
Yeve yow holy myn hert, myne owne knyght, be ye sure.
And to love yow best only as myne owne hert dere,
Wythowte repentauns, I take yow fully for my fere. *companion (spouse)*

"And he that an hows fyllyd wyth gold had yovyn me,   *house*
1130 So joyful schuld noght me a made, trost yt veryly, *have made, trust*
As yowre wordys have done; but sythyn that ye   *since*
Purpose to be trwe, I sqwere to yow feythfully
That ever as trw and as stedfast to yow I schal be,
As ys possyblyl, bothe in weltht and eke adversyté."

1135	And Amoryus than so joyful he myght noght speke	*then*
	But wepyng stylle for this nwe aqweyntauns,	*acquaintance*
	Save at the last thus he sayd, "Lady, and my hert schuld brek,	*even if my*
	I must nede wepe for yowre trwe and feythful plesauns.	
	But wold to Venus," quod he, "that nowe in this happy chauns	
1140	Thys owre the lenght of an hundryd owrys myght be,	
	For to be wyth yow ever is my fulle felycyté."	

"Myne owne knyght," quod sche, "eke yt were myn entent
Ever wyth yow to dwelle; but be yowre provydens,   *wise arrangement*
Ordeyn a tyme nowe, be yowre fulle asent,
1145   Qwan we may have leyser, for the tyme ys now spent,   *leisure*
To speke anowgh; for ful grete sqweme for yowre absens   *enough; sorrow*
I schal have tyl we may mete ayen.
Set ye an owre, and I shcal kepe yt, serteyn."

"Alas!" quod Amoryus, "and must we nedys depart cumpany
1150   So sone? qwy nyl noght fortune us now socoure?   *will not*
But trwtht yt ys that evyl tungys be ever redy;   *truth; evil gossip*
And qwat men wold sey yf thei aspyid us in this owre,
It ys oncerteyn; therfore, betyr yt ys, I knowe yt veryly,
Penauns to sofyr for a tyme than ony maner of susspycion   *rather than*
1155   Schuld ryse of owre asstray walkyng or communycacion."   *[secret] talk*

Thus aftyr, as tellyth the proces of this story,   *narrative*
They endydd thayre delytful communyng   *conversing*
Of ther nwe aqweyntauns, as I have teld by and by;   *told*
And Amoryus prefyryd an owre of ther metyng   *offered*
1160   In the same place; and at her sqwemful departyng,   *sorrowful*
Iche to odyr put thru the crany for a remembrauns
A ryng of gold, for trw lovys everlastyng contynuauns.

And than Amoryus thus sayd, "Madame, for yowre sake
To this walle I do my observauns,   *ritual worship*
1165   And of yow, my lady, my leve I take."
And than he kyssyd the walle, seyng, "For yowre remembrauns   *recollection*
And very tokyn of love wythowte varyauns,   *variance*
Thys insensybyl thyng I kysse insted of yowr persone";
And Cleopes dyd the same, ful sqwemfuly makyng her mone.   *complaint*

1170 Thus thei departyd for aftyr ther nwe aqweyntauns,

   Yede to her beddys joyful of that mery morghtyde,   *morning*

   Kastyng in her mendys to and fro thar lovely dalyauns. *minds; dalliance*

   But the more that thei musyd yt, the more scharply yt gan glyde, [1]

   Thys sperkyl of love, to throwe alle odyr thyng asyde

1175 For only that yt causyd; but aftyr this metyng,   *[love] alone causes that*

   To Palamedon come this mervulus tydyng:

   Masyngerys were sent fro the cyté of Dorestere,

   The qwyche marchyth upon Medys the regyon, *borders; the realm of Media*

   Bryngyng tydyngys that fereful were to here: *hear*

1180 Of an huge and an orybyl dragon,   *horrible*

   The qwyche, as thei made relacion,

   Had destroyd her catel, and eke an hundred men of the cyté *their property*

   He had etyn, besyde odyr harmys don in the cuntré:

   "The qwyche dragan 'serra' men calle,

1185 That wyth hys breth hath enfectyd wyth sekenes   *sickness*

   Nere of alle yowre cyté, bothe gret and smal, *Almost; rich and poor (everbody)*

   That nowe yowre pepyl for thought and hevynes *So that; anxiety; distress*

   So dyscumfortyd be that but ye wul her nede redres,   *unless*

   They wul alle flee and leve yowre cyté desolate.

1190 Ther stavys stond evyn at the yate."   *walking sticks stand; gate*

   And Amoryus alle this wordys of ther talkyng

   Perseyvyd wele, but noght he sayd tyl hys fadyr had spokyn.

   "Qwat sey ye?" quod Palemedon, "dare ye take this thyng? *undertake*

   Be wele avysyd, for yt ys no chyldys pleyng *Consider it well; child's play*

1195 To fyght wyth sqwyche a devyl; for yf yowre wepyn brokyn *weapon*

   Were in fyght, ye were but ded, thowe ye had for certeyn

   As myche strenght as to an hundred men myght perteyn."

   "Fadyr," quod Amoryus, "yf ye wul, I schal asay   *assent; try*

   In specyal for yowre wurchyp and salvacion of the cyté. *Especially; honor*

1200 I fere noght to fyght therwyth, ner never schal say nay *with it; nor*

   To assay myself; for yf yt posybyl be

   Me to overcome yt, the wurchyp schal be to me

---

[1] *But the more they mused about it, the more painfully it burned*

68

And to yow eke, for of Amoryus men wryte schal
That he a dragon dyd sle be hys manhed in specyal.   *courage*

1205   "And yf yt fortune that he sle me in owre fyght,
        The pepyl schal say that, 'Amoryus
        Qwyt hym for owre salvacion as a manful knyght   *Proved*
        That so manful was to fyght for us.'
        Qwerfore, be myn owne conseyt, I deme yt thus: *opinion; conclude*
1210   That bettyr I myght noght dye to have a remembrauns   *[better] remembrance*
        Than in sqwyche a case or sqwych a chauns."   *such a circumstance*

        "Welle," quod Palamedon, "ye wul do yt, yt semyth veryly.
        Spede yow in hast, sythyn ye wul asay,
        And purvey yow of sure harnes in hy.   *armor; quickly*
1215   It stondyth yow an hand wysely yow to aray."   *It behooves you in any case*
        "Myn harnes," quod Amoryus, "redy ys this day,
        And the sunner that Y be forward, the soner thei comfortyd schal be   *sooner*
        That now in gret fere abyde in yowre cyté."

        Anone, in the courte was proclamyd that Amoryus
1220   Had takyn on hand to fyght wyth a dragoun,   *undertaken*
        For in hast Palamedon had comaundyd thus:
        That the most manful of housold to this forsayd town
        Schul Amoryus convey; and thus, wyth a ful conclusyon,   *final decision*
        Thyse masyngerys yede to rest, glad of this promys,
1225   And thus deseverryd; and endyd this entrete ys.   *departed; entreaty*

        Qwan nyght come and iche man was in rest,
        Amorius wele had in mend that this nyght
        He muste wyth hys lady mete for fulle ernest.   *because of [his] ardent passion*
        And to the crany he yede, and fond ther Cleopes bryght
1230   Abydyng hym, mervelyng, as he had trowth plyght,   *Awaiting*
        Come noght; but at the last, ther thei met in fere;   *[He had] not come*
        And aftyr ther comunyng of love, he told her this matere: *discussion*

        Howe he had take on hand to fyght wyth a dragoun,
        And nedys he must erly take hys jurney,   *early*
1235   And howe the masyngerys were sent fro that regyon
        To hym in specyal. "Alas!" quod Cleopes, "for sorow I dey.   *die*

69

Ye ar but dede, for bettyr ye were to fyght wyth a lyon
Than wyth a serpent; for plate ner haburgun   *armor nor chain-mail*
May avayle yf he onys hys venym on yow throw.   *once; venom*
1240   Ye schal dey, never odyrwyse trow.   *believe*

"But qwat serpent ys yt? qwat do thei yt calle?
For sum more esy be than sum as in fyght,   *in respect to battle*
And lesse hurtyth the venym of one in specyal   *in particular*
Than of anodyr; and wysdam wul that ye schuld be dyght   *another; dressed*
1245   In sure harnes theraftyr; for clerkys wryte, of gret and smal,   *accordingly*
Her namys and naturys, and qwerein thei noy be kend natural,[1]
And eke remedyis ayens ther dedly noyauns,   *remedies; harm*
If the case dyd yt reqwire to make wyse purveyauns.

"For of summe of thise serpentys, the eyn so venymmus be   *eyes*
1250   That wyth her loke thei slee yche erthly creature,   *slay every*
As thise cokatrycys; and yit remedyi ys ther, perdé.   *yet; par Dieu (by God, indeed)*
For wyth a wesyl men yt destroye be kendly nature   *weasel*
And the serpent clepyd draconia — that more ys in qwantyté   *size*
Than ony best on erthe, thow he be noght venymmus —   *beast; venomous*
1255   The myght of hys tayl the grete elevaunt sleth most mervulus,   *elephant slays*

"Ayens hos powere, men for an efectual remedy
A panterys skyn bere; and yf thei therwyth schuld fyght   *panther's*
Wyth the venym of a tode or of arany,   *toad; spider*
They sone yt slee; and the serpent namyd jaculus — in hys flyght
1260   Qwat that he uppon fallyth so venymusly, he doth yt smyght   *strike*
That forthwyth yt deyth; and yit a ston ys ther   *dies; stone*
That the serpent may noght hym noght dere.   *[the possessor] dare not [strike]*

"The name of home serpentyne ys; and eke odyr sundry   *which serpentine; types*
Of odyr serpentys so contraryus be to owre nature,   *contrary*
1265   That aftyr summys bytyng or styngyn, men sodenly   *some one of those serpents'*
Falle starke dede; but thei that fere thise chauncys to endure,   *those who travel*
That in desertys must walke, thei purvey wysely
Remedyis of erbys and stonys, as I schal telle yow in hy.   *herbs; stones; in haste*

---

[1] *and how they do harm according to their nature*

"And besyde thise, ther ys a dragon huge and cumbrus,   *troublesome*
1270   Namyd aspys, most to be feryd for hys sotelté;   *guile*
  For enchauntement ner sleyght most ingenyus   *nor cunning trick*
  Can noght bryng hym fro hys den for no necessyté;
  For wele he knoweth hys blode ys medycynabyl,   *medicinal (antidotal)*
  He lyith in hys den a-daylyght ever onmevabyl.   *unmovable*

1275   "But at evyn, yf he hap to mete wyth ony creature,   *in the evening; happens*
  The venym owte of hys tayle into hys mowth
  He drawyth anone, be kendly nature,   *according to its innate nature*
  Thow yt gretly be mervulus and oncowth.   *Though; strange*
  He, or a man beware, throwyth yt fourty fote,   *before; throws it*
1280   Ayens the qwyche plate of stele may noght bote.   *deliver from peril*

  "For as wax ayens the fyre meltyth, on the same wyse   *next to fire; in*
  Steele and yryn be dyssolvyd at the touchyng of that corrupcion.
  Qwerfore, men this profytabyl gyse   *practice*
  Use: a drynk of jacynctys and orygaun   *hyacinth and wild marjorum*
1285   The qwyche thei drynk for ther salvacion
  And anoynte ther skyn, to the qwyche this venym hurtyth no more   *which*
  Than dothe leuke watyr or the fome of a bore.   *lukewarm; foam; boar*

  "And besyde thise rehersyd, ther be in the see   *described; sea*
  Mervulus dragonnys and monstrys also;
1290   As thise chyldrynys, ydrys, and ypotamys ther be,   *(see note)*
  Hos bytyngs be curyd wyth the egestyon of bolys; and odyr mo   *others*
  Dragunnys on erth ther be, but one in specyal most foo   *inimical*
  To alle lyvyng thing — but to man most in specyal —
  The qwyche an hundred fote ys longe, tayle and alle.   *feet*

1295   "And serra cornuta yt ys namyd be clerkys."
  "O!" quod Amoryus, "lady, that same dragun yt ys
  That I schuld fyght wyth, orybyl and furyus in werkys."   *horrible; behavior*
  "In gode feyth," quod Cleopes, "and so hye Jovys me wyss,   *high Jove instruct me*
  I schal noght gab at alle, but telle yow the trwthys: *chatter; truth*
1300   Strenght of man alone may noght prevayl wythowte charmys
  Ayen this serpent; qwerfore, but ye be reulyd be me,   *unless*
  Thow ye were as myghty as Sampson, ded ye schuld be."

"Yys, lady," quod he, "noght only in thyngys prosperus   *auspicious*
Redy Y am to obey, but eke, thow they were to me contrary,
1305   At yowre commaundement in chauncys ryght aventurus
My lyfe for yow in juberté to put; qwy schuld I vary?"   *jeopardy*
"Wele," quod sche, "undyr this forme than do ryght thus,   *plan*
As I schal teche yow; and for no fere yt forgete,   *fear*
For yf ye do, ye schal ther yowre lyfe lete.   *lose*

1310   "In the begynnyg, loke that yowre harnes be sure for onything,   *ready for*
And abovyn alle curyd wyth rede.   *covered; red*
And on sted of yowr helme, set a bugyl gapyng;   *(see note)*
A bryght carbunkyl loke ther be set in the forhed.   *ruby*
And in yowr hand, halde that ylke ryng   *same*
1315   Wyth the smaraged that I here delyveryd yow this odyr day.   *emerald*
Loke that the stone be toward hys eyn alwey.   *eyes*

"And at the begynnyng of your bateyl, loke that ye drynk
Thyse erbys wyth wyne and the poudyr of thise stonys.   *herbs; wine; powder*
Thus thei be namyd — loke that ye upon them thynke:
1320   The fyrst ston orytes namyd ys;
The secunde, lyguryus; the third, demonius; the fourth, agapys;
The fifth, acates; and that ye schal noght fayl of thise same,   *lack*
Send to Walter jwellere be this tokyn in my name.

"And thise be the erbys, be schort conclusyon: *without further ado*
1325   Modyrwort, rwe, red malwys, and calamynt mownteyn,   *rue*
Orygannum, fenel, and dragannys; thus be opyn demonstracion,   *clear*
This confeccion of erbys and stonys, for certyn,
So sure maketh a man — as thei that have prevyd yt seyn —   *safe; tried; say*
That alle venymmus thyng fleyth fro her breth   *flee; their aroma*
1330   In so myche that the water of ther mowth scorpyonnys sleth.   *To such a degree*

"And yf a man were bytyn so that he schuld dye   *bitten*
Of dragon or serpent, or poysunnyd yf he were,   *poisoned*
And onys a sponful of this confeccion he myght ocupy,   *once; take for his own use*
Yt schuld porge hym that never yt schuld hym dere.   *purge; so that; harm*
1335   Therfore loke that ye use this, and I dar sey savely   *salvifically*
That ye schal come hole and sound wyth victory;   *whole*

And aftyr qwyl ye lyve, be had the more in reputacion.
Thys ys the fulle sentens of my counsel and conclusyon." *meaning*

And than Amoryus her thankyd a thousand fold,
1340 Besechyng her to telle qwy hys harnes red schuld be, *armor*
Supposyng that the coloure schuld make the serpent more bold. *Thinking*
"Yowre mocion ys ryght goode, trwly," quod sche, *question (requiring an answer)*
"For sum bestys, as the sey, more wod thei be *beasts; enraged*
Qwan thei se rede, as thise elefantys and odyr many;
1345 But trwly serra, that serpent, red ferytht naturally. *fears*

"And qwy yt ys that ye the bugyl schuld bere? *buffalo*
Thys ys the cause, in fewe wordys I schal yow lere: *teach*

"The bugyl ys to the dragun serra specyal pray,
And qwan the bugyl sethe the serpent, he cryith wyth alle hys myght, *sees*
1350 Knowyng wele he may noght skape awey. *escape*
And qwyl he cryith, the serpent asundyr the bak dotht byte *into pieces*
And aftyr sqwolwyth yt in; and therfore qwan ye schal fyght,
Oon the same wyse he wul asayl yowr portrayd bugyl. *In the same manner*
But there helpyth gretly in the forhed the carbunkyl. *ruby*

1355 "The nyght," quod sche, "pasyth and tomorw ye must ryse erly.
It ys tyme now to go to yowre rest;
For ellys faylyng of slep wul make yow hevy." *Otherwise lacking; sluggish*
And Amoryus than ansqweryd, "Madame, ye say for the best,
But ever my desyre ys to be wyth yow, trwly."
1360 "Veryly," quod Cleopes, "my dysyre ys the same, for trowe ye noght that I
Ful hevy am to departe fro yow — yf yt myght odyr be — *sad; otherwise*
Yis, truly; but wysdam wul to be ware or ther come necessyté." *cautious before*

Thus departyd they as her use was beforn: *their habit; before*
Iche toke leve of odyr, kyssyng on oudyr syde the wal, *the other; either*
1365 Yede to ther rest; and Amoryus erly on the morn
Wysely purveys thise precyus stonys and dyd hem brek smal
In a mortere of bras; and wyth the juse of the erbys alle, *juice*
Made a drynk; and aftyr clad hys harnes in red velwet, *velvet*
And a bugyl of blak corbe dyd set on hys helmet. *raven's feathers*

1370	And hys fadyr had purveyd hym to convey	*provided to convey him*
	Twenti manful men, besechyng Mars them spede.	
	And Amoryus hath taken hys leve, and on hys jurney	*leave*
	He rydyth, and thise masyngerys wyth alle myrth dyd hym leede,	*lead*
	Confortyng hym noght to dreede.	*Encouraging; fear*
1375	"Truly," quod Amoryus, "I fere yt noght, for yf I had,	
	Owte of the cyté ye coude noght me a lad."	*have led*

Thus at the last thei entryd the cyté of Dorestere,
Receyvyd of the mayer and the communnys wyth alle solempnyté   *[And were]*
Possybyl for the tyme; and wyth alle maner of chere   *kindness (solicitude)*
1380   They hym confortyd; that the day he entryd the cyté,   *thus the day*
Fesstful was of the mayre commaundid to be;
And every man that he coude of myrth or pley   *that knew of*
Schuld schewe yt honesté this solempny day.   *suitably; solemn*

Qwan pasyd was the tyme of mete, Amoryus the knyght   *a meal*
1385   A servaunt commaundyd to the mayer to go in hy,
Enformyng hym how he purposyd that same nyght
To take hys vyage wyth the dragoun fyght fully —   *adventure*
Owdyr manfuly to bryng home the vyctory,   *Either courageously*
Or, aftyr fortune for the pepyllys savacion,   *according to; salvation*
1390   Be manhod to dye, as ther alterhyers champyon.   *their greatest*

And qwyl this masynger yede on this masage,   *mission*
Alone in hys chambyr, fro the top to the too   *toe*
He anoyntyd hym therwyth, aftyr werryurrys usage;   *according to warriors' custom*
And aftyr usyd hys drynke and made hym redy to go,   *afterwards; himself*
1395   Armyd on the most sure wyse, and gan walk to and fro,
Abydyng hys masengere; and for he come noght redyly,
He toke hys steed, chargyng that forthte no man schuld hym gy.   *conduct*

And in the myd cyté, as he rod thru the strete,   *middle of the*
The mayer and the pepyl wyth hym mett.
1400   And to the mayer he sayd, "Farewelle, mayere, for I wul mete
Thys nyght wyth yowre enmy; I wol noght let   *forsake [the battle]*
At this tyme for owdyr; at onys I wold yow releve,   *for anything; immediately*
Or to dye for yow in this mysery and myscheve."   *misfortune (evil plight)*

And than this mayer and thys odyr folkys alle
1405 Aftyr gan wepe for thise wordys pitously,
Seyng, "Sythyn that ye this day fyght schal,
Let us go wyth yow and wyth yow dyi;   *die*
Or ellys aftyr fortune bryng home the vyctory."   *else*
"Nay," quod Amoryus, "that were noght my worchyp; that schal noght be.
1410 No creature but I schal go owte of this cyté.

"For sythyn that I only am sent to this entent,   *Because*
I be myn one schal bothe the sqwete and the soure   *on my own; sweet*
For yow endure; and ye that be here now present,
Drawyth yow to the wal or to sum toure,   *tower*
1415 And prayth to Venus and Mars omnipotent,
To Fortune eke; for yowre welfare and prosperyté
Is in my vyage yf I may vyctor be."   *mission (voyage)*

Aftyr that word he prekyd hys steede owte of the toune   *pricked (hurried)*
Into the feld qwere this mervulus dragon lay,   *field*
1420 Wyth schynyng skalys, in vale or an eld dungun,   *scales; old dungeon*
A lytyl besyd the hy way.   *beside; highway*
And fro afer qwan he that serpent sey,   *from afar*
Hys phylatery wyth hys drynk he gan take,   *safeguard*
Anoyntyd hys harnes wythowte and gan alle redy make.

1425 And Cleopes ryng forgate he noght,
But to hys fyngyr he bond yt surely;   *bound it securely*
Wyth hert ful devoute to hys goddys he sought
Hym to defend; aftyr gan up lepe fersly   *protect*
On hys steede and toward the beest he gan hy.
1430 But of the dene of hys steede this dragon gan awake,   *But [because] of the din*
Lyft up hys hed and a mervulus cry gan make.

Than Amoryus, as fast as he myght he dyd hym hy,
Or the serpent rose, yt to wound
Wyth hys spere; but the dragon sone yt gan aspye.   *quickly*
1435 Aloft wyth hys wyngys reisyd fro the grounde
Hys hydus body, and turnyd hym round   *hideous*
Wyth gapyng mouthe as thow he at onys   *once*
Schuld hym at the begynnyng devour both flesch and bonys.

	But Amoryus sqwyftely wyth hys scharp spere	*swiftly*
1440	Wythin the mouth so sore yt gan smyghte,	*vigorously*
	That yt brast and left half there;	*broke*
	And sqwyftly he drw hys sqwerd bryght,	*drew*
	Defendyng hymself as a manful knyght.	
	But the dragon, more wode aftyr than before,	*enraged*
1445	Lepe on hys stede and kylde yt wythoute more,	*Leapt; killed it instantly*

That Amoryus on fote must nede fyght   *So that*
But as yt appyd, be fortune, in hys fallyng,   *happened*
Wyth the poynt of hys sqwerd he smet oute the syght   *struck*
Of the serpentys one eye; and ever he held Cleopes ryng
1450   Ayen the todyr wyth the stone; and wythowte taryng   *other*
He lept aboute, hewyng on on every syde: *cutting away at*
Wyth huge strokys hys sqwerd on the skalys gan glyde.   *descended swiftly*

But ho, trow ye, than was aferd but this folk on the wal   *who; afraid*
Qwan thei sei Amoryus feld and hys steede slayn.   *felled*
1455   "Alas," quod thei, "and cursyd be the owre that this case schul falle   *hour*
Upon yon wurthy knyght; for he comyth no more ayeyn   *won't return*
For manhod, strenght, ner sotel trayn   *subtle trick*
May now noght avayl. Alas! qwy yed he forth alone?
But alle to late now as wantewyttys we make owre mone."   *lackwits; lament*

1460   Thus the ferful folk on the wallys dyd compleyn
Wyth many a salt tere and wryngyng of ther handys.   *tear*
But qwat, suppose ye, that Cleopes feryd? Ye, certeyn!   *feared; Yes*
Sche feryd that he schuld forgete her techyng,   *so feared*
That nowdyr mete, ner drynk, ner odyr thyng   *food*
1465   Myght her comfort for inward fere;
Sche toke yt so hevyly, and at her hart dyd yt bere.   *heart; pierced*

A thousand tymys qwan sche was alone sche gan say,
"My knyght Amoryus, alas! qwat chauns ys thee befall?
I schal thee never more see; qwerfore cursyd be that iche day
1470   That this infortune or juberté schul ever falle." And on the goddys alle
Sche cryid and most to Venus and Fortune in specyal,
"Thy varyabyl squel," quod sche, "O Fortune! brent myght be   *wheel; burnt [it]*
Wyth Pluto in helle, that thus sone hast chongyd owre new felycyté.

"How schal I do qwan I hys fadyr see?   *act*

1475 Brest must my hert, I knowe yt veryly.   *Burst*

The remenbrauns of hys lovely chere so enprendyd schal be   *face; imprinted*

Wythin my hart that I schal nedys dy.

Alas!" quod sche, "qwat onhappy fortune or qwat mysery

Is me betyd that am the most woful creature   *befallen*

1480 Lyvyng on ertht? O Amoryus, Amoryus! how schal [I] endure?"   *earth*

But qwat Amoryus was saf; but oftyn tyme in fere   *Except that; safe*

Herd strokys he had and stynke so orybyl   *horrible*

That had noght hys posyon a be, he had dyid ryght ther   *potion have been; died*

Wythowte wound; for this dragun, as a devyl,

1485 Blwe flamyng venym owte of hys mowth that impossybyl

Was beste or man to lyve that yt onys dyd touche.

I may this wrytyng on the phylysophyr vouche.

And ofte this serpent gan saute the bugyl blak,   *often; assault; buffalo*

The qwyche upon hys helmet stod, and bysyly

1490 Yt beheld; but the ryby so bryght shone in hys ye,

That aferd he was and confusde and ofte turnyd hys bak.   *afraid; confused*

For ever Amoryus the ryng held beforn the face bysyly

Of this dragun and wyth hys sqwerd fast leyd on as doth a smyth   *attacked*

Qwan he a brennyng hote yryn hath upon a styth.   *burning hot iron; anvil*

1495 But alle hys strokys stode to none avayl,

For hys skalys were so hard that noght thei dyd yeld   *scales; yield*

Ayens hys sqwerd; but oftyn wyth hys tayl

He smet Amoryus to the grounde, wyde opyn in the feld,   *struck*

And therto brake alle to pecys hys scheld.

1500 For had noght a bene that precyus ungwent   *salve (unguent)*

He had be slayn and on pecys rente.   *torn to pieces*

But at the last, this serpent, wode for ire,   *crazed by anger*

Gan fersly Amoryus asayle gapyng wyde,   *[its mouth] gaping wide*

Thrwe owte hys venym as flamyng fyre;

1505 But Amoryus yt asspyid and sodenly styrt asyde,   *moved quickly*

And this dragun aftyr sqwyftely gan glyde.   *glided*

But Amoryus, as Fortune wold, to hys pocion —   *took his potion*

Phyal and alle — thrw yt in the mowth of the dragon.   *Vial*

	And forthwyth the mowth closyd as yt had be bound	*as if; been*
1510	Wyth iryn chenys and gan fast to schake the hed,	*chains*
	And aftyr fylle plat on the grounde,	*fell flat*
	Hys brystylyd mosel gan blwe wer as ony led.	
	And qwan yt felt yt schuld be ded,	*it would die*
	Yt gan asay to flye, but in the rysyng	*tried*
1515	Amoryus hys sqwerd to hyltys smet undyr the wyng,	*hilt*

	That yt thyrlyd hys hert and so hevyly	*pierced*
	Fyl doune that as an earthqwave the ground schake;	*earthquake*
	And wyth that set up so hydus a cry	*hideous*
	That the pepyl on the wal for feere gan qwake	*(see note)*
1520	And wythbrast in the myddys and Amoryus hwe of the hed,	*burst asunder; off*
	Levyng that stynkyng body ther sterk ded.	*stark dead*

	And this pepyl on the wal, qwan thei sey	
	Amorys hole and sound, thei lyf up her handys to the fyrmament,	*whole; lifted*
	Iheryng Mars and Fortune; pytusly thei gan sey,	*Praising; piously*
1525	"O blyssyd, O benyngne, O mercyful goddys omnipotent!	*benign*
	Wurchyp and preysyng be to yow that have us socoure sent.	*succor*
	Wyth bollys, rammys, and kydys eke	*bulls, rams; kids also*
	Wythin yowre tempyllys we schal yow feythfully seke."	*seek*

	And wythowte lettyng, doune and owte of the cyté	*tarrying*
1530	Thei yede, and on ther kneys fyl Amoryus before	*fell*
	Wyth dyvyne wurchyppys that wundyr yt was to see.	
	Thys pepylys for gladnes, wepyng more and more,	
	And the mayer and odyr statys that ther wore,	*estates; were*
	A garlond of gold upon hys hed in sygne of vyctory	
1535	Thei empressyd, conveying hym in wyth alle maner of mynstrelsy.	

	Qwat schul I telle the gret presents and that men gan hym yeve?	*tell of; what*
	Sythyn that yche resonabyl wyght	
	May yt conceyve that he that labouryd so for her myscheve,	*their plight*
	They must nedys hym magnyfy wyth alle her myght,	
1540	And hym excellent weryour and most hardy knyght	
	Ever to name qwyl that her lyvys wold endure,	
	To love hym beforn yche erthly creature.	

Thys dragon thus ded, as here ys wrytyn before,
Amoryus schop home hys wey as sone as he myght;   *made his way home*
1545 For the memoratyf dart had woundyd hym so sore
Of Cleopes bryght chere, wyth her frendly wordys qwyght,   *pure*
That alle worldys felycyté was in maner as a derk nyght
To the prime oryent sparkyl of hys daunyng fyre,   *burning desire*
Nwe radyfyid wyth the flame of veneryan dysyre.   *ratified; sexual*

1550 Thus in conclusyon, he toke hys vyage   *journey*
To the cyté of Albynest qwere he ful honorabylly
Was receyvyd of eld and yong of the nobyl lynage.   *lineage*
But qwo was than glad? deme ye rygtly?
Cleopes, I gesse, that in fere was so gretly,
1555 For empres to a ben made sche coud no more joyful a be   *That for; have been*
Than qwan sche hym lyvyng in helth gan see.

O lord! qwat joy that sche had and how myri and glad   *merry*
Sche gan be qwan he wyth vyctory of that serpent   *over*
Was commyn wyth helt! More joy sche had   *in health*
1560 Than Orphe qwan he hys wyf receyvyd ayen for the rent   *Orpheus; recompense*
Of hys musycal melody, the qwyche in helle brent;
More glad than Parys of the rapt of qwene Eleyn   *abduction*
More gladnes in her hart sche had, the soth to seyn.   *to tell the truth*

For clerk wyth penne, or tunge of retrycyan,   *pen; tongue of rhetorician*
1565 Or musyng hert can noght telle half her felycyté.
But alas! this sqwete delyteful love drawyth to the conclusyon.
Of the byttyr, peynful, and scharp endyng adversyté,   *painful*
I qwake for fere to wryte! — yf yt myght odyrwyse be   *otherwise*
Of ther endys! — But that endyter that wul a story take,
1570 He must as wele of the byttyr as of the sqwete mencion make.

But to the proces. Amoryus that nyght determynyd fully   *sequence of events*
To have wyth Cleopes hys lady the lovely dalyauns,   *dalliance*
As thise loverys have the practyk and knowyng fully   *experience; full knowledge*
Of that sqweete and plesaunt observauns.
1575 And as he purposyd — ryght so efectwally
He fulfyllyd in dede — to mete at the walle as thei dyd before.
I trow than veryly that thei bothe myry wore.

79

But to the purpose. Of ther dalyauns, this was the conclusyon:
That thei schuld mete the nest mornyng
1580 In a forest that was fast by the toune,
In a certeyne erbere beforn the dawnyng,   *arbor*
Iche alone qwan no creature were steryng,   *stirring*
And there to breke ther hertys of all hevynes,
Her lovys eke undyr a nwe forme to redres.   *satisfy (see note)*

1585 Thus thei departyd to ryse erly,
Yede to ther rest in fulle very trost
The nest morw to expend ful delectabyly   *spend*
In lovys observauns, noudyr to spare for snowe ner frost.
Bysyly thei gan record ther speche that no tyme schuld be lost,   *rehearse*
1590 That thus and thus thei schul say — but alas that yche qwyle   *all along*
Dysseyvabyl Fortune gan hym dysseyve and begyle!   *Deceiving*

But trwth ys sayd that God schapyth for the best.
He knwe at the begynnyng qwat the conclusyon schul be.
And to telle forth this story: qwan thei woke of ther rest
1595 Thei gan them fast aray qwan thei gan se
The dauns of the systyrrys sevyn
Drawe toward the west part of hevyn.

But eight days beforn apperyd in the fyrmament
A lemyng sterre that a comete ys clepyd in astronomy   *gleaming star*
1600 In the mylke qwyte gyrdyl; that ever doth represent   *(i.e., the Milky Way)*
A gret chaunge, as the deth of princys, or pestylencys gret and hasty,   *sudden*
Gret bataylys, deth of kyngys, or gret penury,
The qwyche the same morw gan dysapere   *(i.e., the comet)*
That this case fylle as I wryte nowe here.

1605 In this morw, erly before the day,
Cleopes ful privyly at a posterin yate   *secretly; postern gate*
Stale owte alone and to the forest toke her wey;   *Stole*
For in her thowt sche feryd to a comyn to late   *feared to have come*
And fast sche gan her hy in her jurney   *hasten*
1610 Toward the erbere; and qwan sche come and se no creature,   *garden*
"A!" quod sche, "I fyrst am comyn, now am I sure."

Amoryus and Cleopes

And in this erbere, as seyth my boke, ther was
A lusty, fresch, delectabyl spryng of water clere,
The qwyche ran smothly thru the chas   *hunting ground*
1615 Of this forest owte of this foresayd erbere.
And Cleopes qwan sche sey Amoryus come noght nere,
To the water sche yed and wysch bothe handys and face,   *washed*
And her dryid and fast abowte gan gase.   *gazed*

And as sche lokyd about, sche aspyid comyng
1620 An huge lyon, the qwyche that nyght to hys pray   *for*
Had devouryd an hyinde; and aftyr hys fedyng   *hind*
Erly come to drynke of that fresch spryng.
And Cleopes, ny fro herself for that soden afray,   *nearly beside herself; fright*
Fled away as fast as sche myght renne,   *run*
1625 And for fere styrt into a lyonnys denne.   *escaped*

And as sche ran, a kerchyf pynnyd losely   *pinned*
Fyl fro her hed awey upon the gres,   *Fell; grass*
But for gret hast sche dyd yt noght aspy.
And forth into the erbere this lyoun come wyth mowth al blody;
1630 But or he drank, aftyr hys nature, he gan hym dres,   *cleaned himself*
Wypt on the gres hys blody mowth, and in hys welteryng   *wiped; rolling about*
Made alle blody Cleopes kerchyf in hys wypyng;

And aftyr rose up and dranke of the water hys fylle;
Aftyr into the forest he yed be anodyr wey,   *went by another*
1635 But Cleopes for fere lay ston stylle.
Sche lokyd alwey to a ben the lyouns pray.   *thoroughly expected*
And Amoryus nas noght longe, but wythoute delay   *was not*
Hyid hym as fast as he coude; and for sureté   *safety*
Hys sqwerd undyr hys arme he bare for case of adversyté.

1640 But alas! qwy nas yt broke on pecys thre   *three pieces*
Thys ylke sqwerd but qwat Fortwne wold so?   *same; except that*
It was ther desteny; yt wold none odyr be   *not otherwise*
But Amoryus and Cleopes must dye therwyth both to.   *two*
Qwat schuld I yt prolonge? Y must be ordyr go   *Why*
1645 For ony ther chauncys; and so Amoryus entryd the erbere,   *In spite of*
And thus it befyl as ye schal aftyr here.

81

Qwan he was come to the erbere, fast he gan loke

If Cleopes had owte be styryng ther ere.   *been; earlier*

But sodenly he abaschyd and fyl into fere

1650   Qwan he this blody kerchyf sey lying there.

Hys hert gan cold and hevy wax os ony led: *as lead*

"Thys ys Cleopes kerchyf," quod he, "in peyn of myn hed."   *on pain of my death*

And forthwyth he stoupyd and up the kerchyf gan take,

And lokyd uppon the merke and fond for Cleopes a C,   *mark*

1655   Wrowt wyth sylke; than evyn as an espys lef doth schake   *aspen*

Ayens the wynd, ryght so than dyd he,

Dyd qwake for fere qwan he that lettyr gan se;

And at the fyrst word thus pytusly he gan crye,   *piteously*

"O, hye Jovys help! help! for now I dye."

1660   Encrese so sore began hys inward hevynes,

That as a lyoun wode for ire ryght so he faryd   *crazed by anger; fared*

Nygh owte of hys mend; and in that gret dystres   *Nearly; mind*

Hys inward conseyt thus he had of Cleopes   *notion*

Wyth mornyng hert and pytus chere; thus he hys conseyt declaryd:

1665   "O most trosty, most trw, most lovyng!

Cursyd be that owre that we gan trete of this metyng.   *hour; discuss; meeting*

"For this ys trwth, experyens schewyth yt opynly;

And be this blody kerchyf I yt deme   *discern*

That for very trw love sche keme hydyr ryght erly   *came; hither; early*

1670   Me to abyde — alas, for sqweme!   *grief*

And sum lyoun or tygyr come here forby,

The qwych for hys pray hath drawen her to hys cave.

Alas! qwy nas I here her to save?   *why was I not*

"O fers! O crwel! O wod, ravenus best!   *mad ravenous*

1675   Was ther none odyr pray to sufyse thi gredynes,   *ravenousness*

Of hert or hyinde or odyr best walkyng in this forest

But on that lovely mayd, my lady Cleopes?

O hye Jovys! inclyne thine ere, or that myne hert brest,   *ear before; bursts*

To my prayur; that as the thundyr dynt slow Companeus,   *thunderclap; slew*

1680   Ryght so this crwel best myght dye that was so ravenus.

"Or ellys, or my woful spyryt owte of the body pase,
I myght wyth that vermyne mete to venge Cleopes detht. *revenge; death*
And yf yow nyl me here, thi brodyr I pray of grace, *will not*
That Pluto men clepe wyth hys fyry breth. *fiery*
1685 As at the sege of Thebes Amphyorax fro hys place
Fyl into helle alle qwyk, ryght so this foule best and vermyne
Myght falle thorw the erth to helle pyne." *hell's pain*

And at that word, the cramp so sore gan hys hert hold
That he nyst veryly qwat to sey; *did not know truly*
1690 But sodenly he gan to syghe, as hys hert brest wold. *sigh as if*
And at the last cryid, "Allas and welawey!
Alas! how schal I doo? for sorow I dey.
O hert myne, Cleopes! O myne hevyn sqwete!
Alas! qwy schal I never more wyth yow mete?

1695 "Alas! that I in prime love thus beraft of my gladnes; *the beginning of love*
And yyt a mayd never lovyd but one, *yet*
The qwyche Fortune wyckyd hath slayn gylteles. *guiltless*
Allas! I — sorowful wrecche, wythowte comfort, alone — *wretch*
Nowe schal dye; and now to yow Furyis infernal, I make my mone: *Furies*
1700 O thow helle hound Tricerberus, opyn thi yatys wyde, *gates*
And conjoyne my spyryt onto my lady syde. *unite; unto; lady's*

"For sythyn Fortune nolde us sufyr here *since; would not forbear us*
To mete in felycyté, I must wyth sorowful hert ende
Owre love begunne; for sche for me hath bought yt dere,
1705 And Y as dere yt schal yeld that I onkend *yield; faithless (undutiful)*
Never schal be found in bodé ner mend. *body*
Lo lytyl spryng! to thee I compleyn wyth hert sore;
Ther schal never lyvyng creature wyth me speke more."

And wyth that word hys sqwerd owte he drwe,
1710 Wyth crwel chere and scharp voys gan sey, *fierce*
"Farewele, knyghthed! farewele, aventurys nwe!
Farewele, lykyng lust! farewele, alle myry cumpany! *pleasurable desire; merry*
Farewele, beute! farewele, fame and vyctory!
Farewele, alle lykyng dalyauns of alle worldys felycyté! *pleasurable dalliance*
1715 Farewele, myrth, welth, sporte, and pley, for alle ys pasyd wyth me!"

And wyth that word he lete downe glyde   *swiftly descend*
The pomel of hys sqwerd, and held the poynte aloft,
And aftyr yt set to hys left syde
Wyth ferful and grysely chere thise wordys rehersyd ofte: *repeated often*
1720 "O Cleopes, my lady dere! my spyryte nyl nowt abyde,
But nedys yow folw, how sore sumevery smert!"   *each and every pain*
And wyth that word — alas! — he smet hymself to the hert.

And in that crwel dede, so loude he cryid, "Farewele, Cleopes!"
That sche hys voys herd and styrt owte apase   *quickly*
1725 Of this denn; but alle to late sche gan her dres,   *took her course*
For qwan sche come, he lay grovelyng on hys face.
And qwan sche aspyid that very onhappy case,
Sche wept and wrange her handys, and sayd thus pytusly:
"Alas! myne owne knyght, qwy dye ye thus schamfully?"   *shamefully*

1730 And betwene her armys sche lyft hym aloft,
And to hym sayd, "Alas! ys this oure metyng?
Ys this the love that we have musyd so oft?"   *contemplated*
And qwan he herd her voys, hys hert gan spryng
Wyth hors voys, as myne autour tellyth hys dying,
1735 Amoryus her teld that he went be her kerchyf blodye   *supposed*
Sum best had her devouryd, "This is cause that I thus dye."

And Cleopes that word so sore toke to hert
That as an ymage of stone ryght so wythowte myght   *strength*
Sche fyl on sqwounyng; and longe tyme aftyr up sche stert
1740 Fro dethys crampe, and Amoryus upward had turnyd the qwyght *white*
Of hys eyn; this Cleopes than the most woful wyght
That myght bere lyfe qwan sche sey hym ded:
Her chekys sche gan tere, and rent the here of her hed.   *lacerate; hair from*

And wyth that sche cursyd Fortune and the goddys alle,
1745 As sche that lost had alle worldys felycyté,
And gan to sey, "O!" quod sche, "sythyn that I dye schalle,
Qwerto prolonge I the tyme? sythyn yt must nedys be   *Why*
That I schal dye, for I knowe never more to se
Hym lyvyng ayen, that for my sake ded ys,
1750 I were to onkend aftyr to lyve, iwys."   *too unnatural (faithless); surely*

And wythowte more, sche gan kysse the ded body,   *without more ado*
And aftyr seyd, "O, Saturne! thee I bescche
The soule of this knyght in thi spere deyfy.
And eke be now oure soulys leche;   *physician*
1755   For hys love, on myself now I schal wreche.   *inflict vengeance*
Conjoyne owre spyrytys, qwedyr thow wylt wyth joy or peyn;
For now I folowe, thow I be lothe to deyn."

And Amoryus sqwerd than owte of hys grysely wound
Sche drwe owte; and thus aftyr sche gan sey,
1760   "O onhappy sqwerd! thow schalt me confound   *destroy*
That fleemyd hast the lyfe of thi lord this day.   *driven out*
Cursyd be the oure that thow were made, and weleawey!   *hour*
O Jovys! my vyrgynyté to thee I sacryfyse in this nede,
Wyth the roseat blod of pure maydynhede."   *roseate; maidenhood*

1765   But sythyn yt yrkyth me to wryte   *irks; describe*
The dethys of bothe, I pase schortly.   *I pass over them briefly*
But Cleopes for certeyn herself dyd smyte   *strike*
Thorow the body — alas, that sche so schuld dye!
But alle this was but wrechydnes and foly.
1770   Thow that in eld tyme paynymmys yt dyd for a memoryal,   *ancient times; pagans*
I yt commend ryght noght at alle.

Thus thise storyis as thei fylle, as be my rudenes,   *lack of learning (skill)*
Bothe of her love and of ther sqwemful ende,   *sorrowful*
I have wrytyn; and now to the folwying proces   *series of events*
1775   I my rude style in hast redres.   *address (set right)*
Alle be yt so that I have noght redy in mend   *Even though it be that*
The termys of retricyannys that so freschly schyne;
And thow I had, the tyme sufyse noght them to combyne.   *Even if*

The Prolog into the Laste Boke

O Sunne of Grace that fro the hevynly trone   *throne*
1780   Descendyst into this world! alle of Thi benygnyté   *graciousness*
Becomyng man, alle thise errourys to fordone,   *errors; put an end to*
The qwyche illumynyst synderesys of mannys sensualyté,   *conscience of man's*
Namynd be ryght *oryens sol justycye*,

85

Incomprehensybyl Thi wysdam and domys be fynally,   *judgments; ultimately*
1785   That doyst and fordoyst, dysposyng alle to that ys necessary.   *creates; destroys*

The bemys of Thi wysdam yevyng to thi chyldyr dere,   *beams*
Wythdrawyng them qwere that thei may noght schyne,   *shine*
As fro the hertys of them that worldely wyse appere;
That eke of Thi infynyte godenes fully to fyne   *end*
1790   The thralle bond of Adammys gylt Thi magesté dydyst enclyne
In servisabyl forme apperyng, us to geyn by   *i.e., physical (human); gain*
Soferyng the most schamfull deth — upon the cros woldyst dye.

And that the world schuld knowe Thee to be savyd endelesly,   *in order to be*
Wondyrrys Thow wroutyst mervulusly in oure nature,   *i.e., in human form*
1795   Alle sekenes relevyng, and yit more wondyrfully,   *sickness*
Ded bodyis makyng to lyve, that yche creature
Schuld wurchyp Thee for God, wyth hert pure;
And to Thi trw servaunts yevyng power, more specyally —   *preeminently*
For strenght of Thi doctryne — to reyse many a ded body.

1800   Qwerfore, O eternal God! alle wurchyp and preysyng be to Thee   *worship*
Of hevynly, erthly, and eke infernall.
And yche creature in hys nature bothe on erth and in see,
Qwedyr yt lyvyth wyth spyryte or grennes, in generalle,   *(see note)*
And eke alle Thi handywerkys, bothe gret and smalle,
1805   Myght yeve Thee preysyng; and I now of Thi hynes   *highness*
Beseche Thee up this story to redres.

[Here Endyth the Prolog and Begynnyth the Laste Boke]

Amoryus and Cleopes thus ded, as I rehersyd before,
Yt happyd be the dyspensacion of God that mornyng
An holy man to pase farby, hos name was Ore,   *at a distance*
1810   That an hermyte was, had in that forest hys dwellyng,   *hermit*
Gadyrryd that morw wyld applys to hys lyvyng,   *Gathered; wild*
Hard the scrykyng of Cleopes qwan sche dyid,   *Heard; shrieking*
And to wyte qwat yt was, thidir fast hym hyid.   *know; hastened*

But for the qweyntenes of the fend,   *cunning; fiend*
1815   The qwyche for fraude dothe make sqwyche cry

Amoryus and Cleopes

To inquyete holy lyverys to wythdrawe ther mend *disturb; pious people; mind*
Fro prayyere and contemplacion, this holy man broute to mend.
Or he yed, therfore, he made hys prayyere devoutely, *Before he approached*
Besechyng God yf yt were for the best to abyde or go,
1820 He myght have knowyng qwat were beste to do.

And as he lay in hys prayyer plat on the ground, *flat*
A soden lyght come fro hevyn and therwyth a melody,
Makyng so mervulus a melody and so sqwete a sound,
That he half raveschyd was be the sqwete armony. *ravished; harmony*
1825 And therwyth a voys soundyd, the qwyche bad hym hy *voice; orderd*
Thydyr he was ment for the soulys savacion *salvation*
Of the pepyl of the cyté and eke of the regyon.

Thys voys pasyd and this forseyd lyght, *ceased*
And this holy man rose hym to go.
1830 And qwan he come nere and perseyvyd that ferful syght, *perceived; fearful*
Gretly he was dyscomfortyd tho, *aggrieved then*
And fast gan cast in hys mend to and fro
Qwat was best to do; and be hys revelacion,
He construyd that bothe were paynymmys be the conclusyon. *by inference*

1835 And wyth that he fylle on kneys and up hys handys gan hold *fell*
Toward the fyrmament, besechyng God of hys benygnyté, *graciousness*
Of hys hye mercy eke, that he wold *high*
Hem turne to lyfe yf thei krynsnyd wold be. *christened*
"For blyssyd Jesu Thow wotyst wele," quod he, *know*
1840 "That I onwurthy am for my synful lyvyng
To beseche Thee of this gret mervulus thing.

"But I beleve if Thow wyl them restore
To lyfe ayen, the pepyl of all the cyté,
Bothe men and women, lesse and more, *i.e., everybody*
1845 Schal fully be convertyd and leve in Thee. *believe*
Now blyssyd Jesu, graunt yt may so be, *grant*
As Thow dyidys for alle mankend, *died; mankind*
To redeme them that thralle were to the fend. *enslaved; fiend*

    "And O Qwene of Mercy and Modyr Dygne!   *Mother Worshipful (i.e., Mary)*
1850 Trone of God, my ful trost ys in Thee,   *Throne*
    That comfort art of alle carful; Mayd most benygn,   *full of care; Maiden*
    Synguler joy and refute in every necessyté,   *Singular; refuge*
    Be now my voket — as my trost ys Thee —   *advocate*
    To Thi blyssyd Sone, for noght he wul Thee deny
1855 That Thou besechyst fore; I knowe yt veryly."

    And wyth that this holy man gan upryse,   *rose*
    Yede to Cleopes, fast wepyng,   *weeping profusely*
    Drew owte the sqwerd on the best wyse
    He myght, for more hurtyng   *to prevent*
1860 Thys wound allewey fast bledyng.   *continually*
    Undyr this forme and lyke manere,   *According to this method and fashion*
    He reysyd thise bodyis, and ye schal now here: *raised*

    "In Hys name," quod this eremyte, "that boute mankend,   *hermit; bought*
    Kryst Jesu, yowre soulys into yowr bodyis
1865 Entyr may ayen, fro the powere of the fend.   *away from*
    And thow I be noght wurthy of my merytys,   *(see note)*
    Hole and sound, wythowte wemme of yowre woundys, *Whole; injury (blemish)*
    Nowe upryse, and yeve Hym preysyng wyth hole hert
    That delyveryd yow hath fro peynys smert."   *sharp pains*

1870 And wyth that word, bothe deede bodyis upbrayd.   *arose*
    And wyth o voys thei gan thise antune of Owre Lady,   *one; anthem*
    Evyn as of one mowth and tunge yt had besayd;
    And ever thise wordys they gan multyply   *repeat*
    Wyth many a tere that ran fro ther ye,   *eyes*
1875 And pytus voyse, thei sange, "*Salve, salve,*
    Salve, salve, regina mater misericordye!"

    That ys to sey, "Heyl, qwene and modyr of mercy!"
    Thus thei her preysyd wythowte sesyng,   *ceasing*
    Tyl this holy ermyt axid hem qwy   *asked*
1880 That thei contynwally rehersyd that preysyng.   *repeated*
    They ansqweryd that ther soulys, dampnyd in fyre everlastyng *damned*
    Amonge the fendys, at Maryis commaundement   *fiends*
    Were delyveryd and to the bodyis sent.   *set free*

Amoryus and Cleopes

      "And eke yowreself us semd that ye ther were, [1]

1885   And for us prayd to the Lord, that for alle

      Dyid on the cros; and hys angel this dyd us lere,   *teach*

      To preyse hys modyr as Empres Celestyalle,

      Byddyng us ever for a memoryal   *Ordering*

      Thys orysun to sey in presyng of that blyssyd Lady,   *prayer; blessed*

1890   That sche ondeservyd schewyd us her mercy. [2]

      "Qwerfore," quod thei, "for Hys sake that us dere hathe bougth,   *dearly; bought*

      Make us Krystyn and teche us the wey ryght   *Christian; way*

      To serve that Lord; for nowe we dowght nowght   *doubt*

      That God is none but one that regnyth in hevyn bryght.   *reigns*

1895   For alle tho that we beforn dyd wurchyp, apperyng godys to owre syght,

      Dampnyd spyrytys be in helle everlastyngly

      That have us begylyd be vanyté and foly.

      "For alle thise goddys Hys creaturys be,

      And noght thei may do wythowte hys sofyrauns,   *sufferance (forbearance)*

1900   That owre myschevus ende hath now browt to felycyté."   *unfortunate*

      "Wele," quod this ermyght, "than fully be ye

      In purpose to forsake alle the custum and governauns

      Of paynymmys secte, and now yf ye this forsake,   *pagans*

      I schal yow baptyse and Krystyn make."

1905   And anone, he gan hem lerne; and teld hem in the begynnyng   *teach*

      How this world faryth as a feyre, ever onstabyl;   *fares; fire*

      And how that deth ys oncerteyn, and qwat peyne ys at the endyng;   *unpredictable*

      And qwat ther reward schuld be of joys incomperabyl

      For sofyrrauns of thise transytory thingys onstabyl;

1910   For Cryst seyth that ful streyt yt ys   *difficult*

      A wordely wyse man to entyr hevyn blysse.   *worldly; heaven's*

      And of alle odyr thingys necessary,

      Thys ermyght enformyd them fully in the feyth   *hermit; faith*

      And baptysyd them in that welle ryght devoutely

1915   And aftyr, as myne autoure Fyrage seyth,

---

[1] *And also it seemed to us that you were there*

[2] *Who showed us, undeserving, her mercy*

Thys ermyght axyd of qwat stok thei come, and qwy   *asked; lineage*
Thei had so fordone themself, and how thei come into that place.   *killed*
And thei teld hym, as I rehersyd before, alle the case.

"Now trwly," quod this ermyght, "gret pyté yt had bene   *pity*
1920 That to so semly personys so schuld a dyid;   *two so seemly*
And more pyté the los of yowre soulys to have sene,
But vertuus love of God was never denyid."
And this qwestyon this ermyte axid,
"Is the love," quod he, "as gret now as yt was before,
1925 Or owdyr yt ys lessyd, or yt ys more?"

"For my parte," quod Amoryus, "as longyth to me,   *as pertains to*
My love was never greter to this lady
Than yt ys at this owre, ner greter yt may be."   *nor*
"How thinkyth yow?" quod the ermyte to Cleopes, "sei your fantesy." *tell*
1930 "I am," sche seyd, "so God plesyd be, wyth hert, wyll, and body,
Goddys and this knytys; and qwat fortune so-every endure,   *whatsoever*
Never to forsake hym for none erthly creature."

"Wele, dere soulys," quod this holy man, "yt ys Hys wylle
That hath yow restoryd to lyfe that this mervelle
1935 Be schewyd in the cyté, and for this skyl: *revealed; reason*
That the pepyl schuld Hym knowe that haruyd helle.   *harrowed*
And for this cause Y yt yow telle,
That the pepyl of the cyté for this myrakyl crystyd schal be,   *miracle; christened*
Qwere ye aftyr the lawe despousyd schal be."   *married*

1940 But in this menetyme, myche sekyng ther was   *meantime; seeking*
Aftyr Amoryus qwan he that day dyd noght appere;
For Palamedon thru the cyté dyd enqwire of more and las   *everyone*
Qwedyr Amoryus was gone; and on the same manere
Thei enqwyrryd aftyr Cleopes fare and nere,
1945 But nowdyr were founde; that causyd ther fadyrys care
That no man coude telle qwydyr thei schuld fare.   *go [to find them]*

Thus the rude pepyl wyth privy langage ran to and fro   *unlettered; furtive*
Wyth qwysperyng speche, "A! quere ys he, and qwere ys sche?
Benedycyté! qwat eylyd them thus awey to go?"   *Gracious!; ailed*

Amoryus and Cleopes

<table>
<tr><td>1950</td><td>But be Palamedonnys assent, yt was commaundyd in the cyté</td><td></td></tr>
<tr><td></td><td>That alle the communnys redy schuld be</td><td>community</td></tr>
<tr><td></td><td>In the tempyl of Venus to wete be revelacion of ther goddes</td><td>to know</td></tr>
<tr><td></td><td>Qwere were becomyn Amoryus and Cleopes.</td><td>had gone</td></tr>
</table>

<table>
<tr><td></td><td>And qwylys the pepyl in the tempyl lay in prayyere,</td><td>while</td></tr>
<tr><td>1955</td><td>Thys holy man entryd into the tempyl,</td><td></td></tr>
<tr><td></td><td>Brynggyng wyth hym Amoryus and Cleopes; and to the spere</td><td>sphere</td></tr>
<tr><td></td><td>He toke hys wey, and wyth gret voyse cryid among the pepyl,</td><td>loudly</td></tr>
<tr><td></td><td>"O blynd pepyl! qwy knele ye here?</td><td></td></tr>
<tr><td></td><td>Qwy forsake ye yowre maker almyghty</td><td></td></tr>
<tr><td>1960</td><td>And wurchyp this devyl? qwy do ye this foly?"</td><td></td></tr>
</table>

<table>
<tr><td></td><td>Than this pepyl gretly astoynyd; but qwan thei sei</td><td>were astonished</td></tr>
<tr><td></td><td>Amoryus and Cleopes ther, thei yede nere.</td><td></td></tr>
<tr><td></td><td>But fyrst, Palamedon and Dydas to ther chyldyr dere</td><td></td></tr>
<tr><td></td><td>Yede in hast, wythowte more delay,</td><td></td></tr>
<tr><td>1965</td><td>Enqwyryng qwere thei had ben alle that day.</td><td></td></tr>
<tr><td></td><td>And this ermyght toke this speche on hand boldely,</td><td>undertook</td></tr>
<tr><td></td><td>And teld them alle the chauncys by and by.</td><td></td></tr>
</table>

<table>
<tr><td></td><td>But qwan he reportyd how thei were dede,</td><td></td></tr>
<tr><td></td><td>And eke schewyd the tokynnys of ther woundys,</td><td>tokens</td></tr>
<tr><td>1970</td><td>The pepyllys chere gan change, and pale as ony led,</td><td>grew pale</td></tr>
<tr><td></td><td>And than to syghe and wepe and to wryng ther handys.</td><td></td></tr>
<tr><td></td><td>But qwan he teld the myrakyl, folwyng aftyr tho wordys,</td><td></td></tr>
<tr><td></td><td>That the God of Krystemen had schewyd them Hys godenes,</td><td>Christian men</td></tr>
<tr><td></td><td>The hertys of alle the pepyl gan enclyne, both more and les.</td><td>rich and poor</td></tr>
</table>

<table>
<tr><td>1975</td><td>"But wulle ye wete," quod he, "qwat yowre goddes ys</td><td>know</td></tr>
<tr><td></td><td>That Venus ye clepe? — for certeyne, a devyl of helle.</td><td>call</td></tr>
<tr><td></td><td>I schal schew yt yow alle, so God me wys,</td><td></td></tr>
<tr><td></td><td>And so yeve credens to that I telle.</td><td></td></tr>
<tr><td></td><td>And this spere that mevyth thus fast, in an eyschel</td><td>eggshell</td></tr>
<tr><td>1980</td><td>I may yt put; for thow yt seme gold and schynyth rychely,</td><td>although</td></tr>
<tr><td></td><td>Alle ys but a sotelté of the fend to blere yowre ye."</td><td>subtlety (trick); blur; eye</td></tr>
</table>

Wyth this worde, the pepyl gan schoute and wyth one voyse say,
"Performe thi wordys, and anone we alle

Convertyd to thi lord schal be and krystynnyd this day."

1985 So this ermyght of sylens than dyd them pray   *silence; request*
And he hys wordys schuld performe alle.
Thus he spake, as hys wordys I reherse here,   *spoke*
Fyrst to the ymage of Venus and than to the spere:

"O blynde spyryte, most envyus aungel of elacion,   *pride*
1990 Most froward and fals, that fyllyst fro hevyn for thi presumcion,   *who fell*
That thus longe hast japyd the creaturys of God be fals simulacion;   *deceit*
Thow orybyl, nakyd spyryte! in the vertu of Hys passyon
That bought mankend, breke nowe thi mansyon —   *dwelling*
Thys ymage of Venus — that be opyn demonstracion
1995 The pepyl may thee se that thow hast blyndyd beforn
To thi utyr schame, confusyon, and sckorn."   *utter shame*

Thys word nas sunner spokyn but tht the devyl gan owte flye   *was no sooner*
And brake the ymage on pecys and ther odyr goddys alle;
And therwyth made sqwyche a noyse and sqwyche a cry
2000 That alle the pepyl for fere to the ground dyd falle.
And he commaundyd the spyryte that no creature at alle   *person*
He schul noy, but to a desert qwere no creature were abydyng   *annoy*
Hastyly to pase, ther to the day of dome to make hys abydyng.   *judgment*

And therwyth he seyd to the pepyl, "Qwy ly ye so?   *lie*
2005 Yowre grete enmy ys fled; ryse up and se
More mervellys yit; for or we go,   *before*
Thys fantastyk spere fordone schal be."   *destroyed*
And wyth hys hand he bekynnyd the pepyl, bad them come nere.   *urged*
"Fere ye noght, and here qwat I schal sey;   *Fear; hear*
2010 And put fro yowre hertys alle doutys awey."   *doubts*

And so the pepyl dyd; and he in opyn audyens
To the spyrytys thus seyd that mevyd the spere: *moved*
"O dysseyvabyl spyrytys, qwy make ye resystens   *deceptive; resistance*
Ayens yowre Makere? qwy dysseyve ye that He hath bought dere?
2015 But envye causyth yt, for that ye wold in fere   *Except that; together*
Them have dampnyd wyth yow in everlastyng fyre.
I knowe that this ys yowre entent and yowre dysyre.

"Qwerfore, that alle this pepyl may knowe opynly
That ye hem dysseyve, this fantasye and ye now dyspere
2020 In Hys name that sofyrryd the Juys Hym crucyfye;   *suffered (allowed)*
And schew opynly that this fantastyk spere
Is no thing materyal, but as the smoke of a fere."   *fire*
And noght soner this word was spokyn,   *sooner*
But this spere was vanyschyd and brokyn.

2025 And noght apperyd — noudyr gold, sylver, ner precyus stone;
But spyrytys fulle the tempyl, wyngyd lyke larkys;   *filled*
And qwan the pepyl sei the spere was vanyschyd and gone,
"Thys ys innowe," quod thei, "we beleve alle thi werkys.   *enough*
Anone us krystyn make, wythowte delay, everychone."   *everyone*
2030 And this holy man the spyrytys commaundyd to wende   *go*
Owte of the tempyl, the qwyche bare yn ther gate the chyrchys end [1]

And than this holy man gan them lere   *teach*
The feyth of the chyrche, and towght them fully
To serve ther Maker qwyl thei were lyvyng here,   *i.e., while they were alive*
2035 Tellyng them the peynys of helle and eke the glory
Of hevyn, promysyng them that blys to possede everlastyngly   *possess*
If thei the commaundements of God kept; and than them alle
He crystynnyd — men, women, and chyldyr, both gret and smalle.

Thus was the profecye fulfyllyd of Venus, as be revelacion   *prophecy*
2040 To her secretary schewyd, as I rehersyd before,   *revealed*
How that a crucyfyid man schuld take possessyon,
And Venus and her felyschyp to exclude for evermore;   *fellowship*
The qwyche ys Cryste, crucyfyid of Juys, made ther hys mancion   *Jews*
Qwan thei crystynnyd were and the tempyl dedycat,
2045 Venus uttyrly excludyd and Jesu fully possescionat.   *having possession*

Thus hath this sqwemful morw a yoeful evynyng.   *grievous morning; joyful evening*
Qwan this pepyl wyth gladnes home schuld wend,   *go*
Browte this ermyght into the cyté, myryli syngynge,   *merrily singing*
To Palamedonnys palyse, qwere he prayd them, at the end,   *palace*
2050 The neste morw to come to chyrche, and for this enspecyal: *especially*

---

[1] *Out of the temple, which in their departure created the church's final purpose*

Amoryus and Cleopes

To joyne Amoryus and Cleopes be lawe matrimonyal.

Thys pepyl of tho tydyngys replete wyth joy and gladnes
Of that soden and hasty begunne maryage;   *sudden; hastily*
For most convenyent thei thowt that Cleopes —   *suitable (proper)*
2055 Aftyr ther consyderauns — was bothe of beuté, byrth and lynage   *consideration*
To be Amoryus fere; for bothe thei were of one age.   *[Fit] to be companion*
"And sythyn," quod the pepyl, "he wul her to wyve take,
Lete us tomorow alle joy and myrth make."

So this pepyl yed home to ther reste;
2060 And on the morw, on the most solempne wyse,
They hem arayd, and to the palyse the worthyest
Of the cyté yede to brynge to chyrche, aftyr the gyse,   *custom*
Bothe Amoryus and Cleopes; and qwat the pepyl coude devyse
Of solempnyté or sport nas noght to seke —
2065 That possybyl was for schortnes of tyme — to eke.   *to increase, add to*

Wyth alle melody that myght be found aftyr the usage   *custom*
Of that cuntré, thei led were to chyrche and of this ermyght
In the tempyl despousyd; and eght days contynwaly aftyr the maryage *wed*
Were kept in solempnyté and fest to the derke nyght.   *feast; until; dark*
2070 To ryche and pore that wold come or myght,   *For*
And to the dwellerrys of the same cyté,   *And for*
The fest was continuyd the mountenauns of wekys thre.   *duration*

And aftyr, this erhmyght ordynyd — the pepyl to lere —   *hermit ordained; teach*
Prestys and clerkys to serve God contynwally;   *Priests*
2075 And thei, stedfast in the feyth — he commyttyd them to God so dere.
And to the forest qwere he wunnyd he gan hym hye,   *dwelled*
Days of hys lyfe expendyng in prayere solytary,
Ever preyng for prosperyté of the pepyl in the cyté,
Tyl hys soule up fley to eternal felycyté.   *flew*

2080 And Syr Amoryus ever encresyd in goode fame,
Also in manhod, in joy, honour, and tranqwyllyté
Wyth Cleopes hys lady; for ever ther gret love was the same
As in the begynnyng, for ever ther owdyrys felycyté   *each of their*
Was iche in odyrys presens fore to be.   *other's*

94

2085	And many beuteus chyldyr thei had that rychely	*beauteous children; richly*
	Were beset, havyng lordechyp of the regyon successyvely.	

And aftyr longe felycyté, Amoryus and Cleopes on one day
Yeldyd ther spyrytys to God; and togydyr in a grave
Ther chyldyr them byryd in a tumbe of marbyl gray,   *buried; tomb*
2090   Platyd wyth ymagys of gold; and superscrypcionys thei have
Into this day, as he that red them sqwore, so God hys soule save,   *Unto; read*
In the tempyl was and red the scrypture that wrytyn ys   *[Who] In*
In langage of Percys and in Englysch; yt ys this: *Persia*

"Flowre of knyghthod, to the world a memoryal
2095   Of trosty love, Syr Amoryus resstyth here,   *faithful*
Defensor of the cuntré, keper of pes contynwalle;   *Defender; peace continually*
And be hys syde, Cleopes, hys lady dere,
Byryid ys — exsampyl to alle women, fer and nere,   *far and near*
Of trwelove, stedfastenes, and curtesy;
2100   Upon hos soulys almyghty God have mercy."

Thys ys ther epytafy, wrytyn at ther fete,   *epitaph; feet*
In a plate of laton, and yche notabyl dede   *brass; deed*
Of hys bateylys and howe he wyth Cleopes dyd mete   *battles*
Gravyn be ther eke, that thei that can may them esyly rede   *Engraved*
2105   For a gret remembrauns; and thus this story I owte lede,   *conclude*
Mervelyng gretly that noght nowe, as in eldtyme,   *old times*
Men do noght wryte knyghtys dedys nowdyr in prose ner ryme.   *write of; deeds*

But qwedyr encresyng of vexacion yt causyth onlye,   *only*
Or defaute of cunnyng, wyth odyr causys moo,   *more*
2110   I can noght deme; but I trowe, yf men ther wyttys lyst to applye,   *determine*
They myght in Englond, and odyr cuntreys mo also,
As notabyl storyis of manhod and chyvalrye   *courage*
Of knyghtys now lyvyng as of them before a hundred and two yere;   *(see note)*
And rather thei schuld fayle endytyng than matere. [1]

2115   And in Englond many notabyl knyghtys ther be
In sundry placys, but of one I make remembrauns,

---

[1] *It is the failure of their writing rather than [a lack of] matter [about which to write]*

The qwyche lyvyd in my days in gret prosperyté

In este Ynglond; the qwyche for prudent porte of governans,   *self-conduct*

And knyghtely behavyng in Marcys chauns,   *Mars' chance (i.e., war, battle)*

2120   Wurthy ys in the world to be preysyd wythowten ende   *without*

Of wryter and endyter for oblyvyon of mend.   *[to prevent] oblivion*

But trwth yt ys that a gret rootyd tre   *tree*

Durabyl frute beryth; of this knyght, I mene, nobyl of lynnage,   *lineage*

The qwyche decendyth of a gretyd aunsetré   *honored ancestry*

2125   Of nobyl werrourrys that successyvely, be veray maryage,   *true*

The to and fyfty knyght ys computate to hys age, [1]   *two*

Home God hath induyd wyth alle maner of sufycyauns   *Whom; endow; ability*

So dyscrete therwyth that abyl he ys an hole reme to have in governauns.

Wysdam ever settyng in yche werk before, [2]

2130   As Salomon in *Sapyens* makyth remenbrauns;   *The Book of Wisdom*

Prudens hys frend and systyr he namyd evermore,

Wyth hos counsel he so demenyd hys governauns   *ruled his conduct*

That iche wyse creature hym lovyd wyth hertely afyauns.   *unrestrained trust*

Ever as a wurthy werryur in every necessyté   *warrior*

2135   Hym qwyt for hys knyge, bothe on lond and see;   *He proved himself; land*

As at Waxham, qwere Gyldenerrys londyd to brenne the cuntré,   *burn*

Thys excellent knyght bare hym as a champyon.

And the hole matere that lyste to rede and see,   *who it pleases*

Rede the story that I endyght of Kyng Cassyon;

2140   And in the ende ye may yt fynde — aftyr the destruccion

Of Corbellyon — qwere I alle hys notabyl dedys bryng to remembrauns,

Done wurthyly of hym in Englond and Frauns.

And ye that this story can noght fynde,

Seke them in the begynnyng of Alexander Macedo,

2145   Or in Josue, or Josepus, for in thise storyis I brynge to mende

The knyght Mylys Stapylton and hys lady bothe to.   *both two*

Now here I spare yow that yt be so. [3]

---

[1] *[Who] up to his era [generation] is reckoned to be fifty-second in direct descent*

[2] *[Stapleton], setting wisdom before all [other concerns] in each task*

[3] *I now here spare you from a similar story of the Stapletons*

I have of hys dedys many to wryte;
I purpose in odyr placys in specyall them endyghte.

2150 But this knyght despousyd had a lady, *married*
Havyng decens be ryght lynage *direct, legitimate lineage*
Of that wurthy and excellent stok lyneally *in a direct line*
That Poolys men clepe, to duke Wylyam as be cosynnage
Ryght nece;[1] that of Sufolk fyrst successyvely
2155 Was bothe fyrst markeys and duke; and be this remembrauns *marquis*
Ye may noght fayl qwat kyng had than Englond in governauns. *fail to know*

And fore that thei — the qwyche be nowe onborne —[2]
Qwan this lady ys pasyd, schal rede this story, *has died*
That thei for her schal pray on evyn and morne,
2160 I alle the storyis that I endyght. I wryte this memory: *compose; [for] this*
That be here lyve thus sche was namyd communly *In accord with her behavior*
Modyr of norture, in her behavyng usyng alle gentylnes, *nurture*
Ever redy to help them that were in troubyl and hevynes.

So beuteus eke and so benyngn, that yche creature *beauteous; benign*
2165 Here gretly magnyfyid, commendyng her womanhede *Her; extolled*
In alle her behavyngs, ireprehensybyl and demure;
And most to commende that of thoughte:[3] sche toke gret heede
To the necessyteys of the pore, relevyng them at every nede.
Of her beute and vertuys, here I sese; for yt ys so, *cease*
2170 I hem declare in Crysaunt, and odyr placys mo.

And yf I the trwthe schuld here wryght,
As gret a style I schuld make in every degré
As Chauncerys of qwene Eleyne or Cresseyd doht endyght, *Chaucer's*
Or of Polyxchene, Grysyld, or Penelopé. *(see note)*
2175 As beuteus, as womanly, as pacyent as thei were wunt to be, *accustomed*
Thys lady was, qwan I endytyd this story,
Floryschyng the sevyn and twenty yere of the sext Kyng Henry.

---

[1] Lines 2153–54: *That men call the de la Poles; according to kinship, / The direct niece of Duke William [though they were actually first cousins]*

[2] *And in order that they — who are yet unborn —*

[3] *And to commend that [quality of hers] most in remembrance*

Go now, lytyl boke; and wyth alle obeychauns,   *obeisance*
Enterly me comende to my lord and mastyr eke,   *Entirely*
2180   And to hys ryght reverend lady; wyth alle pleasuns,
Enformyng them how feythfully I hem beseke   *beseech*
Of supportacioun of the rude endytyng owte of Greke.
For alle this wrytyng ys sayd undyr correccion,
Bothe of thi rymyng and eke of thi translacion.

2185   For thei that greyheryd be, aftyr folkys estymacion,   *gray-haired*
Nedys must more cunne be kendly nature   *know; naturally*
In yche syens qwere — in thei have ther operacion —   *science*
Sythyn that craft comyth be contynwauns into every creature —   *persistence*
Than he that late begynnyth; as be demonstracion   *recently; as is demonstrated by*
2190   My mastyr Chauncerys, I mene, that longe dyd endure   *Chaucer*
In practyk of rymyng; qwerfore profoundely,   *practice*
Wyth many proverbys, hys bokys he rymyd naturally.

Eke, Jon Lydgate, sumtyme monke of Byry,   *formerly*
Hys bokys endytyd wyth termys of retoryk,   *rhetoric*
2195   And half chongyd Latyne, wyth conseytys of poetry,   *conceits*
And crafty imagynacionys of thingys fantastyk;
But eke hys qwyght her schewyd and hys late werk   *white hair*
How that hys contynwauns made hym both a poyet and a clerk.   *poet*

But nowe thei bothe be pasyd, and aftyr schal I;   *dead*
2200   Qwerfor I make this schort orysun: *prayer*
O Welle of Mercy, Jesu, that I be freelnes and foly   *frailty*
Have Thee ofendyd in dede or in ony imagynacion,   *thought*
Fully of foryefnes I Thee beseche wyth my hertys hole entencion,   *forgiveness*
Purposyng to amende alle that I have done amys.   *amiss*
2205   To me, Jesu, now Thi mercy ful necessary ys.

And thei that my sympyl wrytyng schal rede   *read*
Of storyis of elde tyme, yf thei lyste, of ther godenes,   *old times; wish*
Qwere thei Jon Metham in bokes fynde, pray for hym to spede   *to*
In vertuys; for he of rymyng toke the bysynes   *virtues*
2210   To comforte them that schuld falle in hevynes
For tyme onocupyid, qwan folk have lytyl to do,
On haly dayis to rede, me thynk yt best so.   *holy days*

But . . . . there be as in the north cuntré
But he . . . . tok on hand   *undertook*
2215   He nere was borne, as ye in hys odyr bokys may se,   *books*
The toune of Camberig, toward the este of Englond.   *town; Cambridge*
But hys fadyr fully in the north born was he
The qwyche be ryght consangwynyté,   *direct, legitimate descent*
Decendyd fro the fyrst Alyscounder Metham, the knyght,
2220   . . . the lord . . . of payn . . . i . . . travyle . . .,
Wos son it was that endytyd this story,
Preyng the reder of pacyens hertyly. [1]

HERE ENDYTH THE STORY OF AMORYUS THE KNYGHT AND OF CLEOPES THE
LADY

---

[1] *Praying heartily for the reader [to have] patience*

Notes

Abbreviations: **Barber**: Richard Barber, ed. & trans. *Beastiary: Being an English Version of . . . M.S. Bodley 764, with all the Original Miniatures Reproduced in Facsimile.* Woodbridge, Suffolk: Boydell (for the Folio Society), 1993; **Chaucer**: Larry D. Benson, et al., eds. *The Riverside Chaucer*, third ed. Boston: Houghton Mifflin, 1987; **Craig**: Hardin Craig, ed. *The Works of John Metham*; **Trevisa**: M.C. Seymour, et al., eds. *On the Properties of Things: John Trevisa's Translation of Bartholomaeus Anglicus "De Proprietatibus Rerum,"* 2 vols. Oxford: Clarendon: Oxford University Press, 1975; **Whiting**: Bartlett J. Whiting and Helen W. Whiting. *Proverbs, Sentences, and Proverbial Phrases from English Writings Mainly Before 1500.* Cambridge, MA: Belknap Press, 1968.

Manuscript Description

The manuscript of the poem is ruled for twenty-eight lines of text on each page. The decorated initial "T," which begins the text, extends from the first line to the eighth and from the left margin to the center of the text area. It contains the armorial shield of the Stapleton and de La Pole families. A floriated border of painted acanthus leaves frames the text along the top, bottom, and left margins. The top margin of the manuscript has been trimmed. Other initial capitals, two-lines high, occur at lines 1, 71, 232, 248, 325, 724, 1024, 1779, and 1807. Those at lines 71 and 248 also have roughly drawn profiles of grotesque human heads facing the left margin and extending upward into a blank space in the preceding line. The capital "N" at line 724 has some crude, unfinished tendrils extending several lines down the margin. Other stanzas begin with one-line high initials that vary in color and usually extend into the left margin. These serve to mark off the beginning of the stanzas, which in the manuscript are not separated from one another by a blank line as they are in this edition. All the other lines of text begin with a minor capital, and a yellow wash over the initial capital of each line extends vertically down the page.

Headnote. *an hundred.* MS: *C.* So too in lines 502, 1140, 1182, 1197, and 1294.

1–7 See the Introduction. The first stanza of Chaucer's *Troilus* reads as follows:
The double sorwe of Troilus to tellen,

> That was the kyng Priamus sone of Troye,
> In lovynge, how his aventures fellen
> Fro wo to wele, and after out of joie,
> My purpos is, er that I parte fro ye.
> Thesiphone, thow help me for t'endite
> Thise woful vers, that wepen as I write.

8   This line duplicates *Troilus* II.50. The stanza is a conventional description of spring.

13   *Nero*. Nero is not known to have conquered Asia. Perhaps he functions here simply as a figure of tyranny, conquering the world.

14   *Kyng Camsyre*. Craig suggests Darius? (p. 179), or possibly a name formed from *Cam* and *Cyrus* "after the pattern of such words as Cambucean and Cambyses, the first syllable carrying with it some idea of lordship; or it may be an ignorant imitation" (p. 159).

16   *Medys*. Media is an ancient kingdom, sometimes a province of Persia, located in what is now northwestern Iran.

18   *pleyn of Pansopherys*. An imagined space in the exotic East where battles take place; perhaps akin to Persepolis, as Craig suggests (p. 159).

29   In the MS, the initial letter of *that* is a thorn, overwritten with the contemporary *y* form of the letter; a similar emendation has been made to the initial letter of line 37. The scribe writes the *y* form almost everywhere else. (Both types of thorns have been expanded to *th* in this edition.)

35   *too*. MS: *ii* written above *too* or *to*, here and elsewhere, to indicate number, not reduplication. So too in lines 1101, 1103, 1113, 1643, 1920, 2126, and 2146.

40   MS reads *pysauns*, but this is certainly a scribal or authorial error for *Pyramis*, Amoryus' counterpart in Ovid's tale.

44   *Daryus*. Presumably the one time "Camsyre" of Persia and Media. See note to line 14.

45   *Fyrage*. Metham names the fictitious source of his work, Fyrage, here and at line 1915; see the Introduction.

50–54   Metham's narrator casts himself as a imperfect writer needing the editorial help of other writers. This was a common motif in fifteenth-century poetry formed on the model of Chaucer's Parson's Prologue (X[I]55–57) and *Troilus* (III.1331–36).

55–56   Proverbial expressions; see Whiting, T465 and M754. MS: *qwete*. The scribe's normal orthography of modern *sw-* is *sqw-*, as in *sqwete (sweet)* and *sqwerd (sword)*, but in the manuscript the spelling *sqwete* occurs two other times (lines 1566 and 1824) and *qwerd* occurs five times (lines 1497, 1639, 1717, 1758 and 1760). Each of the *qw-* spellings has been silently emended to *sqw-*.

67   *Norwyche.* Norwich, in northeastern Norfolk, was at the time of Metham's writing one of largest and most important towns in England and the site of the episcopal see for Norfolk and Suffolk. The Stapleton family maintained a townhouse in Norwich, about 15 miles from their manor at Ingham.

89   *Tessaly.* Thessaly is a region of eastern Greece, and one of the areas conquered by Alexander the Great.

92   MS: after *sone, and* is marked for deletion.

96–98   In The Clerk's Tale, Chaucer describes Walter as "ful of honour and of curteisye; / Discreet ynogh his contree for to gye" (IV[E]74–75). *Of mene stature* might suggest balanced proportions as well as average size. Criseyde "mene was of hire stature" in *Troilus* V.806.

110   *moreovyr.* MS: *moreovyer.*

        heldyng a frame. Holding a [model of?] a structure, presumably the new temple (*frame*: "a structure of any kind; a framework" [MED]).

125   *dysmayd.* MS: *dysmanyd.*

138   I have retained Craig's reading of *lest,* but the *s* has a cross-stroke and therefore could be an *f.*

142   *aucte.* The *c* is written above the *t.* Craig interprets this as an abbreviation for *-gh,* but *aucte* also occurs at line 427.

Notes

148–52 The comparison of the beautiful heroine to Phoebus, the sun, is conventional. The terms that the narrator here employs — *creature, stature, womanly* — are all words that Chaucer uses to describe Criseyde (*Troilus* I.281–87).

159 *That.* MS: *Tat.*

161 *Mars furyus.* Chaucer uses the same collocation in *The Complaint of Mars* (line 123), though the idea is a commonplace.

163–68 Classical Latin poets, rhetoricians, and their medieval followers advocated brevity as one of the virtues of style, but attestations of brevity often became merely empty formulae in narratives which amplified source material instead of condensing it. See Ernst Robert Curtius, *European Literature and the Latin Middle Ages*, trans. Willard R. Trask (1953; rpt. Princeton: Princeton University Press, 1973), pp. 487–94.

169–75 The poet here has engaged in a rhetorical device for the condensing of narration or description, called *occupatio*, by which he makes an excuse for not writing about something. In typical Chaucerian fashion, the *occupatio* actually does what it claims not to do, in this case elaborate on the construction and fabrication of the temple. E.g., see The Knight's Tale, I[A]2919–66, or The Squire's Tale, V[F]67–68.

172 *as chaudrunnys and fylateryis* (such as cauldrons and phylacteries). Phylacteries are amulets used for protection or repositories for a holy relic (OED 2 and 3).

178 *twenty.* MS: *xxti.* So too in line 1371.

185 *hys hynes.* MS: *hysnes*; I follow Craig's emendation.

186 MS: *wryte* between *this* and *wyse* is marked for deletion.

232–38 Metham invokes the modesty topos, derived from classical authors and a commonplace among medieval authors, including Chaucer and Lydgate. Here Metham uses his dull *poyntel* or stylus for writing or engraving as a metaphor for his unrefined verse. See Curtius, *European Literature and the Latin Middle Ages*, pp. 83–85.

237–38 *Bayard* was a common name for a horse, and "blind bayard" is a proverbial example of foolish pride (see Whiting, B71). Chaucer uses the name several times (see especially *Troilus* I.218–24 for the proverbial use), as does Lydgate.

239   This stanza, which begins with a two-line high capital, is preceded by three blank lines. The result of the blank lines is to make the following pages alike in that each has four complete stanzas per page up through folio 39a.

240   *in specyal.* "in particular." Chaucer regularly uses the term as a component of his empiricism. The singularities (i.e., that which is *in specyal*) are what make discretion possible if the knower is to avoid being lost in the general. See *Boece* V.m.3.

241–45   Chaucer's narrator in *The House of Fame* describes the goddess as arbitrary, like Lady Fortune. For those supplicants to whom she grants fame, Aolus, god of the winds, blows a golden trumpet of praise; either a hellish horn of slander or silent oblivion is reserved for others (*HF* 1559–1688).

249   *Aurora* is the goddess of the Dawn.

250   *ruschyng of a chest.* Craig suggests moving of a chest, but *ruschyng* is also the "noise accompanying rapid movement" and "the rustling of a tree" (OED). The phrase could refer to heavy breathing or perhaps the rustling of a chestnut tree, with *chest* taken as a clipped form for the purpose of rhyming.

250–61   Metham gives us an insight into what amounts to a fifteenth-century night light and clock as well as speculation on strange sounds in the night and ways of reassuring oneself.

259   *appryse.* Possibly a scribal error for *up rise*.

264–65   *Latona* is the mother of Apollo and Diana by Jupiter, though Metham seems to have in mind Diana, the moon, following Chaucer (*Troilus* V.655).

265   *Boetes.* Boötes, the constellation of the Plowman, containing the bright star Arcturus.

266–67   *systyrrys . . . sterrys sevyn.* Both refer to the Pleiades, the cluster of seven bright stars in the constellation of Taurus. According to Trevisa, the sun takes its course by the Pleiades in June, causing rain and "fairnesse of floures" (1:505). Astronomical/astrological treatises of classical origin were increasingly common in Christian libraries from the ninth century on, abetted in the twelfth century by Arabic works. Such treatises often contained diagrams of the universe and illustrations of the figures of the constellations. Nicholas' *Almageste* in The Miller's Tale (I[A]3208) is such a book.

267   *sevyn*. MS: *vii*. So too in lines 463, 599, 606, 909 (with *vii* written over *Sevyn*), and 1596.

270   *fyry goddes*. Venus is the fiery goddess because she seems brightest when low in the heavens just before dawn and because, in her glow, she excites the passions of lovers. See Robert Henryson's celebrated example of her bright and potent beams in *The Testament of Cresseid*, lines 11–28. See *The Poems of Robert Henryson*, ed. Robert L. Kindrick (Kalamazoo: Medieval Institute Publications, 1997), pp. 156–57.

275   *at debat*. "in conflict." Mars and Venus have opposite attributes: war and love, dry and moist, male and female, guilefulness and truthfulness, etc., but Venus is said to abate Mars' malicious influence. According to Trevisa, during months of fair weather, Venus is the morning star and announces the sunrise (1:481–82). In The Knight's Tale (I[A]2438–41), Venus and Mars argue over which of their worshipers, Palamon or Arcite, should win the tournament. See also Chaucer's *Complaint of Mars*, where Mars and Venus abide for a time in the same house and debate why Venus must leave so soon.

277   *this mysery* refers to the medieval commonplace that life in the physical world is full of pain and suffering, relieved only by death and the passage of the soul to heaven. The key treatise on this topic is *De Miseria Humane Conditionis* by Pope Innocent III. See *On the Misery of the Human Condition*, ed. Donald R. Howard, trans. Margaret Mary Dietz (New York: Bobbs-Merrill, 1969).

279   *hevyn crystallyne*. That is, the Ptolemaic universe, envisioned as a series of concentric crystalline spheres containing the seven planets and the stars. See C.S. Lewis, *The Discarded Image: An Introduction to Medieval and Renaissance Literature* (Cambridge: Cambridge University Press, 1967), p. 96.

283–89   *hye Saturne*, the oldest of the gods, is depicted with a scythe, representative of his association with sowing and harvesting. Being furthest from earth (the seventh and slowest sphere, and thus the highest) he is said to have the most baleful effect on human affairs. He devoured all his children except Jupiter, Neptune, and Pluto, and Juno sprung forth from his head. These later gods, of course, represent the four elements.

289 MS: *yow* canceled, *thow* with *th-* rather than the y-thorn written above the line, apparently to clarify the syntax of the clause. One possible example of the past participial prefix, which, when it was not dropped completely in later Middle English texts, was simply *i-* or *y-*, is retained in *iheryid* (lines 289 and 303); but the prefix with the present participle *Iheryng* (line 1524) suggests that this was the scribe's habitual spelling of the word.

298 *the mone* is written above the line.

304–10 *deyfyid sygnys.* The Zodiac, with its twelve equal divisions, each distinguished by a constellation which represents a figure of terrestrial origin, such as a ram (Aries), or weighing scales (Libra), or the Water Carrier (Aquarius), referred to here. The *fyx* or fixed stars include those of the constellations and all others which retain their spatial relationship relative to one another (unlike the seven planets), in the eighth crystalline sphere.

305 *mancionnis.* Mansions or houses are the twelve signs of the Zodiac. Each of the planets has two houses, one day and one night, in which they exert their greatest influence (OED I.8.b).

306 *cateracte* is one of the floodgates of heaven.

307 *poolys.* MS: *polys* with superscript *o*.

311 *colegyat* (collegiate). The sense of *college* was broader in Middle English, not necessarily referring to an educational institution, but "an organized society of persons performing certain common functions and possessing special rights and privileges" (OED 1; see also 2).

314–15 Metham is referring to the influence of planets as they pass through their "houses" of the Zodiac in which they have the most influence (on human affairs), and can consequently be said to "reign" at those times.

318 The line begins with a capital "A," which is canceled. *Alna* is probably for *Al Nasl*, a yellow star in the *Sagyttary*, that is, Sagittarius, the constellation of the Archer, a centaur that stands with his bow aimed at the heart of Scorpio. This star marks the head of the arrow. It appears in the summer sky in the Northern Hemisphere.

319 *exorte*. "Ascendant," in astrology, the "degree of the zodiac, which at any moment (especially e.g., at the birth of a child) is just rising above the eastern horizon" and which was thought "to exercise a special influence on the life of a child then born" (See MED, *exorte*; and OED, *ascendant* B.I.1).

330 *pepyllyng* is from the verb *pipple*: "To blow with a gentle sound, to pipe or whistle softly, as the wind" (OED).

333 *erthe*. MS: *orthe*, with superscript *e*.

339 *palfrey*. MS: *palffraey*.

370 *for of the kalendys ye muse the prime*. *Kalends* is the first day of the Roman month, and *prime* the second of the seven daily canonical services, or generally, the morning hours from six to nine a.m., or the first hour after sunrise.

376 Craig's emendation for the MS *begynne moun cure chauntes*.

381–401 A narrator walking in the woods and overhearing a lover's complaint to Fortune about the loss of his lady is reminiscent of Chaucer's *Book of the Duchess* and Lydgate's *Complaint of the Black Knight*. See the Introduction.

387–88 In medieval cosmology, the goddess Fortune, signifying chance, mutability, and instability, ruled everything under the circuit of the moon, including the physical world and human events. She was usually depicted with her wheel on which humans rise and fall. The key text on the nature of Fortune is Boethius' late classical treatise *The Consolation of Philosophy*. English translations are attributed to King Alfred and Chaucer, and Boethian ideas inform much of Chaucer's writing and that of his fifteenth-century followers as well, usually through Chaucer's translation.

399 *sqwownyng*. MS: *sqwownyg*.

404 *feinere*. MS: *f einere*, the scribe avoiding an imperfection in the vellum between the *f* and the first *e*.

423 Marginal note: *How Palamedon was receyvyd*.

429 Craig expands the abbrevation to *mancion*, but two superlinear marks indicate *-ioun*.

450   Craig misnumbers this line as 451; the correct numbering sequence begins again at line 513 in his edition.

456   *hem*. MS: *he*.

477   *eght*. MS: *viii* (with *eght* written over *viii*). See also lines 692, 899 (with *viii* written over *Heght*), 912 (with *viii* written over *eght*), 1598 and 2068. It is interesting that in *St. Erkenwald*, with which *Amoryus and Cleopes* bears a number of likenesses (particularly in the conclusion), the number eight has a significant function in the renewal of St. Paul's cathedral. Perhaps it is a sign of new beginning here, as well, *be the custummys olde*, this eighth day being a time suitable for the new dedication.

483   Marginal note: *How the nygromancyer with spyrtys made the spere*.

507   Marginal note: *The mervulus werkyng off the spere*.

520   *swyft*. MS: *wyft*.

521   MS marks *in* for deletion.

522–27 *Applanos*, literally, "without a plane surface"; here, a perfect sphere. Craig expands *empor'* to *emperor*, but Metham may have in mind the *celum empireum*, the first and highest of seven "heavens" or spheres named by Alexander the Great in his trip through the heavens. According to Trevisa, the *celum empireum* is a "place of aungels," and the brightest and most shining of the spheres (1:447, lines 454–55). As Craig pointed out (p. 160), Metham is likely working from memory at this point.

523   *Haly* ('Ali) refers to the eleventh-century Moslem astronomer known as Albohazen Haly in Latin translations of his widely circulated work, *The Distinguished Book on Horoscopes from the Constellations*.

532   *dessendyng*. MS: *dessendynd*.

534   *denominacion*. MS: *donominacion*.

535–41 The syntax and the nomenclature make the exact sense of this stanza difficult to determine. *doutyr of Lycaon* is Calisto, a nymph devoted to Diana who had a son by Jupiter. For her transgression, Calisto was transformed into a bear, and later, along with her son, Arcas, into the constellations of the Great and Little Bears, Ursa Major and Minor, respectively. The passage makes more sense if *Artos* is a scribal error for *Arcos* or *Arcas*, that is, Ursa Minor, where the Pole Star is located. *Artophylax*, the constellation of the Bear Watcher, is apparently ready to fight the *serpent*, now generally identified with the constellation *Draco*, which in some manuscript representations envelopes both of the bears in its folds. *Arcton* may be a misnomer for either *Arcas*, as above, or *Arctos*, a common name for Ursa Major. The story of the bears in Ovid's *Metamorphoses* is retold in the *Ovide Moralisé* and by Boccaccio and Gower (*Confessio Amantis* 5:6225–358), and briefly summarized by Chaucer in The Knight's Tale (I[A]2056–61).

542–43   *Adryagne*, that is Ariadne, who fell in love with Theseus and then was abandoned by him after he killed the Minotaur in the Labyrinth. Bacchus took her crown and tossed it into the heavens to cheer her.

544–48   *Hercules* is a constellation represented as standing with one foot on Draco and the other next to Artophylax. It is best seen in the Northern Hemisphere in summer. Representations of the constellation conventionally presented Hercules carrying a club and wearing a lion's skin, but here merely embraces the skin, and the club has given way to the more refined spear or lance.

547   *nynetene*. MS: *xix*.

549   Marginal note: *Off the harp off Orphe with qwyche he harpyd hys wy[f] fro helle.*

549–52   *the harp musycal of Orphé*, that is, the constellation Lyra, or the Harp. In the Ovidian story of the musician Orpheus, the hero enters the underworld and reclaims his dead wife Eurydice by playing his harp, only to lose her again when he looks back, violating Pluto's interdiction. Like the legend of Pyramus and Thisbe, the story of Orpheus was widely known and incorporated in Latin grammar lessons in the later Middle Ages. The story is reworked in the Middle English romance *Sir Orfeo*. See *The Middle English Breton Lays*, ed. Anne Laskaya and Eve Salisbury (Kalamazoo: Medieval Institute Publications, 1995).

553   *sqwan*, that is, the constellation Cygnus. It is associated with the story of Leda, who was impregnated by Jove in the form of a swan.

556   The constellations Cepheus, Cassiopeia, Andromeda, and Pegasus (ridden by Perseus). In Greek mythology, Perseus slew the Medusa, the mother of Pegasus, and

rescued Andromeda, the daughter of Cepheus and Cassiopeia, from a sea monster. Marginal note: *The enamelyngys off the vestyture off goddys*.

557   *Opylenk involvyd wyth a serpent*. Ophiuchus, or the Serpent Holder, a summer constellation in the Northern Hemisphere, is identified with a physician who was so skilled he could bring the dead back to life. "Serpents were always associated [with physicians] as symbols of prudence, renovation, wisdom, and the power of discovering healing herbs" (R. H. Allen, *Star Names and their Meanings* [1899; rpt. New York: G. E. Stechert, 1936], p. 298), and the modern symbol for medicine derives from this.

558–61 The constellation of Aquila, the Eagle, is represented in early diagrams as carrying an arrow. In Greek ornithology, eagles and vultures were often confused; thus, the eagle became associated with the sixth labor of Hercules, to destroy the cannibal birds of Lake Stymphalis. The *dolphyn*, or Dolphin, is Delphinus, a summer constellation in the Northern Hemisphere. *Pegasus* is the flying horse which Bellerophon rode to Mount Helicon, where a kick of the horse caused the spring of Hippocrene, the fountain of the Muses, to flow. *Boyse* is Boeotia, a district in central Greece. The *triangyl* is a constellation just south of Andromeda.

570–76 *Phebus twelve dwellyng placys*. That is, the twelve signs or "houses" of the solar Zodiac: the *Ram*, Aries; the *Qwyght Bole*, Taurus; the *Tweyn Bredyr of Grekys Lynage*: Gemini; the *Crab*: Cancer; the *Lyon*: Leo; the *Vyrgyne*: Virgo; the *Weghtys*: Libra; the *Scorpyon*: Scorpio; the *Sagyttary*: Sagittarius; the *Capricorn*: Capricorn; the *Aqwry*: Aquarius; the *Fysschys*: Pisces.

572   *twelve*. MS: *xii*.

577–83 *the Octyan* is the South Pole. The names of the constellations that follow are generally winter constellations in the Northern Hemisphere: the *Qwalle*: Cetus; *Padus*, the celestial river Eridanus; the *Hare*: Lepus; *Oryon*: Orion; the *sqwyf Grehound, and fers Prochyon*: Canis Major and Canis Minor; the *schyp of Argus*: Argo Navis; the *Centaure or the monstyr of Chyryon*: Centaurus; the *serpent namyd Ydra*: Hydra; the *Pese* (from Anglo-Norman *Peise*): Libra; the *Crow*: Corvus; the *fysch clepyd Serus*: Piscis Australis, the Southern Fish.

591   MS: *h* written in above *owre*.

593   *translat*. MS: *tranlat*.

603 *syngulere.* "Separate from others by reason of superiority or pre-eminence" (OED III. 9).

604 *theyr.* MS: *thereyr.*

608 *syxt.* MS: *vi.*

609 *fyfte.* MS: *v.* So too in line 1322 (*fifth*).

611 *fourth.* MS: *iiii.* So too in line 1321.

617 *thryd trone.* Venus' sphere, the third in the sequence moving outward from earth. Mercury's sphere (line 621) is the second; the moon's (line 622), the first.

618 *Bylyd.* MS has only "B" in the text, but *bylyd* in the left margin.

619 The association here of Mercury with merchants would appear to be based on specious medieval etymology. As the god of eloquence, science, and mathematics, he is useful in persuasion and in the calculating of accounts and, therefore, he is called the god of merchants. Also he is mercurial — quick to appear, and quick to disappear.

624 *clepe.* MS has the past participle marker *i-* written in above the line. Diane is called goddess of the sea because of her recognized power over tides.

625 MS repeats *her*, one above the other.

638 *ye have made.* MS: *made ye have made.*

650 *Nay.* MS: *nay.*

651 *one.* MS: *i.* So too in lines 737, 741, 930, 947, 1871 (*o* with *i* written above), 1872 (*one* is spelled out, with *i* above), 1894, 1982, and 2087.

661 Marginal note: *The vysyon off the secret[ary] off Venus how the spere schuld be destroyd qwan [Christ] schuld take possessyon.*

690 *Cherycos* or Circius, is the northwest wind, though here Metham seems to have in mind simply the compass direction.

705   *slavennys*. A *slavin* is a pilgrim's mantle worn here as a ceremonial robe.

724   This "N" is two lines high, suggesting a major division of the poem.

731   *yed up and downe*. Chaucer often uses similar phrases to describe the hero and heroine in *Troilus and Criseyde*. Troilus' love for Criseyde begins with a similar temple scene, one which Metham follows here in a number of details. See Introduction, pp. 12–15.

736   *fyllyng the champ*, perhaps meaning "filling the open area or field" of the temple, but also possible is "beating the cloth or ground." *fyllyng* may be a spelling variant of *fulling*, "the process of beating or treading on cloth in water for the purpose of cleaning and thickening"; and "to trample down" (MED a., c.). *champ* can also refer to the cloth which forms the ground on which the embroidery is worked (OED sb. 1, 3).

738   Marginal note: *The fyrst aqueynttauns off Amoryus and Cleopes in the tempyl off Venus*.

748   *rolle*. "A quantity of material esp. cloth, rolled or wound up in a cylindrical form" (OED II. 6). Metham has in mind the Islamic practice of kneeling in prayer.

756   *Appollo*. MS: *Venus*.

763   *closet* is a chapel or section of pews reserved for a lord and his family (MED).

771   Nonsense words (*Smsmatm mas m m spm may grem*) make up an eighth line to this stanza, to fill out the 28-line page, apparently made short by an omission in the preceding stanza. Dots underneath the line indicate it should be omitted. Craig prints but does not count this line.

796   A proverbial expression also employed in Chaucer's *Troilus* (IV.936 and 1261–65); see Whiting, W531.

798   *To save her worchyp* (to save her honor, reputation). Cleopes' concern is the same as Criseyde's. See *Troilus* II.468.

800   Marginal note: *Off a straunge conseyt portrayd in Cle[o]pes boke*.

800   *There*. MS: *Hher*

800–06   *hynde* is a female red dear; *hert/hart*: *heart*, but with punning on *hart*, the male red deer, especially after its fifth year when the crown antlers have formed. Conventional allegories of love often employed the female deer as the object of a knight's hunt; see, for example, Chaucer's *The Book of the Duchess*.

803   *on stonys*. This detail is unusual; it likely reflects Metham's familiarity with the mid-fourteenth century tomb of Sir Oliver Ingham (d. 1344) in the chancel of the Church of the Holy Trinity at Ingham. The sepulcher depicts a knight in repose on a ground of rounded cobbles, a motif employed by the same sculptor on two other tombs, one in Repham, Norfolk, near Ingham, and one in Cambridgeshire. Cleopes' book is a pagan version of a Christian devotional manual — a Book of Hours or a Primer — which were common among the upper-class laity by the mid-fifteenth century.

804   *that*. MS: *the*.

        trw lovys. *Herba paris*, a plant with four cloverlike leaves, often associated with pairs of lovers. For elaborate explication of the metaphysical implications of true loves see the popular late fourteenth-century "The Four Leaves of True Love," copied several times in the fifteenth century and printed in Susanna Fein's splendid edition, *Moral Love Songs and Laments* (Kalamazoo: Medieval Institute Publications, 1998), pp. 161–254. Fein includes two illustrations: one, a drawing of the plant itself (p. 163), and a second of a pair of lovers holding true loves (p. 169).

813   *Amoryus yt gan aspye*. MS: *per Amoryus*; see also the note to line 820. The figure of lovers discovering their intentions to each other through a "go-between" book is not uncommon in medieval literature, witness Paolo and Francesca (Dante's *Inferno* V.127–38) reading together that Galetto (pandering) romance of Lancelot; but seldom has the device been used more charmingly than here.

818   *Venus was born foreby*. This describes a processional with a statue of the goddess in imitation of medieval processions of images of Christian saints. Such processions were common throughout Europe before the Reformation.

820   Craig expands the abbreviation to *Amoryus*, but the word is clearly *Peramus* and thus represents a mental lapse by the author or by a knowledgeable scribe.

826   *demonstracion*. MS: *demostracion*.

827   *menyng*. MS: *menyg*.

828   *to and fro* is used several times by Metham; this phrase occurs frequently in Chaucer's *Troilus* and Lydgate's *Troy Book*.

837   *yowr*. MS: *you*. So too in line 1353.

838   *pray*. MS: *play*.

841   *prime*. See above the note to line 370. MS reads *A. Off*.

844   MS reads *but* after *behold*.

858   *a qwarter brede* is a width of cloth, equivalent to 9 inches or a quarter of a yard.

866   *entré*. The ceremonial gathering place for the lists.

868   *place* in this context specifically refers to the open area where the knights engage in the tournament's battles and is distinct from the scaffolding and other areas from which the spectators view the action. Chaucer uses the same term in The Knight's Tale (I[A]2399).

879   *perand*, perhaps a Northern dialectal form of the present participle, has been taken as the aphetic form of *appearing*, but the context here suggest *peering*, "to look narrowly esp. in order to discern something indistinct or difficult to make out," a sense which is not in use, according to the OED, until 1590; but see also the verb *pire*.

883   *emperourys knytys*. MS: *emperour knytys*. So too in lines 886 and 1019. Perhaps the scribe treats the phrase as a compounded noun, in which case emendation is unnecessary.

884   *stagys*. Medieval manuscript illuminations suggest that such scaffolding could be elaborate.

902   *lyklenes*. MS: *lykenes*.

114

915   *knyght*. MS: *knygh*. So too in lines 927 and 1126.

917–18   *coursere* is the heavy, powerful horse used in battle or tournaments; *trappere* is a protective covering of leather for such a horse, probably envisioned here as ornately decorated. *harnes* could refer to other trappings of the horse but probably refers to Amoryus' own armor.

926   Marginal note: *How ther come a knyght aventerus chalengyng to juste with Amoryus.*

940–42   In his challenge, the knight's use of the second person singular familiar pronouns, rather than the polite plural pronouns, indicates his contempt of Amoryus. In line 942, Craig reads *thou* as *you* — either reading is possible — but the singular pronoun suits the context. See line 1842 with similar syntax, and for which Craig renders the initial letter of the pronoun as *th-*.

        alle poyntys of armys. This may simply mean in complete armor, or, alternatively, that the knight wants combat, on horse and then on foot, with lance, sword, and perhaps mace, battle ax, knife, and so forth. His challenge is bold, but in some ways insidious too, in that Amoryus has been fighting all day, first individually, then taking on the whole field, and thus must be near exhaustion.

967   *That over-hasty man wantyd never woo* is proverbial; see Whiting, M97.

970   MS reads *he yt dyd*. Craig supplies *schew* (which I follow), but omits the pronoun.

971   *feld*. In heraldry, the field is "the surface of an escutcheon or shield on which the 'charge' is displayed" (OED II.13.a). The field colors borrowed by the knight were common ones in armorial bearings and would not by themselves indicate the countries in which he fought.

975–80   *rampaund*. In heraldry, *rampant* refers to a beast standing on the left hind leg, with both forelegs elevated, the right above the left, and the head in profile (OED A.1.b). *sabatouns* are armored foot coverings. *Arge* is probably Argos. *passaund*. In heraldry, *passant* refers to an animal walking and looking toward the right side, with three paws on the ground and the right fore-paw raised (OED 4). *grevys*. Greaves are pieces of "armor for the leg below the knee" (OED, *greave* 2.1). *gerundy* or *gyronny* means "having gyrons." In heraldry, a *gyron* is a diagonal line in an escutcheon creating a triangular form, having one side at the edge of the field and the opposite angle usually at the centerpoint (OED). *cuschew* or *cuisse* is a piece of armor for protecting a soldier's thigh (OED).

984–87　*vambracys* are armor for the forearm; *rerebracys* are armor for the upper arm.

996　Marginal note: *How Amoryus dyd slee the knyght aventerus.*

1024　The heading appears as a marginal note; the apostrophic "O" is a two-line-high capital.

1024–28　The exact sense is unclear. The haphazard punctuation of the manuscript is unrevealing, and at the beginning of line 1026 the abbreviation for *That* has been squeezed into the text area. The sense of the passage seems to be that the poet commands the cloudy sky of ignorance to clear, and implores the *precyus modyr* ("precious mother" — in other contexts, an epithet for the Virgin Mary) to sweep the cinders from his eyes that have for too long, to tell the truth, prevented him from achieving the white hair that signifies wisdom. *sky* has several Middle English senses, including the "celestial heavens" and "cloud"; Metham is alluding to the widely circulated *Cloud of Unknowing*, a late medieval mystical treatise. *Aqwilo*, or *Aquilo*, is the North Wind, also known as Boreas, which brings tempests. Metham has in mind Boethius' *Consolation of Philosophy*: "Thus, whan the nyght was discussed and chased awey, dirknesses forleten me, and to myn eien repeyred ayen hir firste strengthe. And ryght by ensaumple as the sonne is hydd whan the sterres ben clustred (*that is to seyn, whan sterres ben covered with cloudes*) by a swyft wynd that hyghte Chorus [the north-west wind], and that the firmament stant dirked with wete plowngy cloudes; and that the sterres not apeeren upon hevene, so that the nyght semeth sprad upon erthe: yif thanne the wynde that hyghte Boreas, isent out of the kaves of the cuntre of Trace, betith this nyght (*that is to seyn, chaseth it awey*) and discovereth the closed day, thanne schyneth Phebus ischaken with sodeyn light and smyteth with his beemes in merveylynge eien (*Boece* I.m3).

1030　The narrator invokes his muse again, the Lanyfica, or Fates; see the Introduction.

1031a　The heading appears as a marginal note.

1037　Amoryus' penance, of course, is owed to Love. Here, and in line 1432, as in other places with the word *knyght*, the scribe leaves the *-t* off *myght*. See note to line 915. Also *bryght*, lines 1066 and 1313, which lacks the *-t*; and *fyght*, in line 1297.

1047   *Syghyng.* MS: *Sygyng.*

1059   Such references to spoken performances appear to acknowledge that literature was often read aloud or recited.

1078   *for sum mystery.* MS: *ssum.*

1085   MS reads *at* for *and²*.

1106   MS reads *o off; this same walle* in a different, smaller hand.

1114   Marginal note: *The fyrst metyng and talkyng betwene Amoryus and Cleopes thru ryvyng off a ston walle.*

1121   *my trwth I plyght* is a phrase which was also part of the marriage ceremony and other contractual agreements requiring an oath of faithfulness, truthfulness, or loyalty.

1153   *knowe.* MS: *kowe.*

1177   Marginal note: *How ther come tydyngs to Palamedon off a mervulus dragon the qwyche dystroyd the cuntre.*

1184–90 *serra.* According to bestiary lore, the serra is a winged sea monster, perhaps a flying-fish, that races ships and tries to becalm them or rip their hulls with its "serrated" crown (Barber, p. 205). Metham's serra is a horned (*cornuta*) variety, and clearly a terrestrial dragon with a poisonous, acid-like venom rather than a fiery breath. The pronouns in this stanza and Amoryus' response in the next indicate that this stanza is a direct address to Palamedon. The *stavys*, staves, indicate the citizens' impending departure; the pilgrim or traveler traditionally carried a walking staff.

1191   *And.* MS: *AAnd.*

1193   MS reads *yᵉow.*

1215   *It.* MS: *In.*

1218   *That.* MS: *Than.*

1228   *for fulle ernest* (because of his intense passion); for an entirely serious purpose; for a complete foretaste (of love) (OED, *earnest*, sb. 1 and sb. 2).

1230   Marginal note: *How [Amoryus] mette the same evyn with Cleopes and teld her howe [he] had take batyel with a dragon.* In the MS, *Palamedon* is canceled, and *sche* is written for *he*.

1238   *plate ner haburgun.* "plate armor nor habergeon," the latter a high-necked, sleeveless jacket of chain-mail armor.

1245   *of gret and smal* is a line filler.

1249   Marginal note: *The kendys off serpentes and remedyiis ayens ther venym.*

1249–52 *cokatrycys* (pl.). Trevisa identifies the cockatrice with the basilisk, a beast said to be able to kill with its fiery breath or with the mere glance of its eyes. It flees from the weasel (which men use against it) because the weasel's bite is fatal to it (2:1153–54). In some bestiaries the basilisk is reputed to hatch from an egg produced by an old rooster, hence the name *cockatrice* and a bifurcation into two animals. Illustrations in medieval bestiaries represent it as part rooster, part snake, which kills the heedless sinner (Barber, p. 185).

1253–55 *draconia.* According to Trevisa, the flying dragon is the largest of all the serpents. Its venom is not fatal; rather it kills its victims with "sawing" teeth and a powerful, constricting tail, which it uses to kill the elephant by binding its feet and strangling it (2:184–86). The dragon is the only animal that flees from the sweet breath of the panther (2:1234); the venom of a poisonous toad is a remedy for other venoms (2:1155). The dragon is allegorized as the Devil (Barber, pp. 183–84).

1255   *myght.* MS: *aight.*

1259   *jaculus.* "a flying serpent. . . . They perch in trees and when their prey approaches, they throw themselves down on it and kill it" (Barber, p. 192). Trevisa likens it to a dart (2:1128).

1267   *thei purvey wysely.* An idea that Palamedon raised earlier, whereby the wise hunter carries remedies with him.

1268   The idea of precious stones having magic or divinely provided powers is an ancient one. Biblical reference to such stones, particularly in Exodus (28:17–21), where Moses commands Aaron to make a breastplate with twelve precious stones, and in Revelation (21:19–21), where twelve stones adorn the foundations of the Heavenly City, were key texts in supporting allegorical interpretations and discussions of their powers. Their attributes were compiled in medieval lapidaries and encyclopedic works like Trevisa's. See, for example, Joan Evans and Mary S. Sergeantson, *English Medieval Lapidaries* EETS o.s. 190 (London: Oxford University Press, 1960).

1269   *cumbrus*. "Full of trouble because of its size" (OED).

1270   *aspys* (pl.). According to Trevisa, the asp is the worst of adders and has the most venomous bite. When an enchanter tries to lure it out of its den, the asp puts one ear to the ground and closes the other with its tail so that it cannot hear the charms. (See Gower's *Confessio Amantis* I.463–80.) There are a number of types of adders, but the dragon adder is not one Trevisa lists.

1272   MS: *ffro hys den* added above the line.

1281   A proverbial expression; see Whiting, W105.

1284   *drynk*. MS: *dryk*.

           jacynctys and orygaun. Hyacinth and wild marjorum, the latter reputed in medieval lore to be an antidote against the venom of serpents.

1290   *chyldrynys* (pl.), a water adder, which according to Trevisa, infects the places where it glides, causing cloudy vision in humans (2:1128); *ydrys* (pl.), hydra, a many-headed water snake, one of which was killed by Hercules; *ypotamys* (pl.), a sea horse beset with scales like a dragon, which, according to Topsell, can fly and has teeth like a swine (possibly confused with a walrus).

1291   *egestyon of bolys* (the dung of bulls); humans bitten by the hydra swell up, but they may be healed by the application of cattle dung (Barber, p. 190).

1295   *serra cornuta*. See the note to lines 1184–90.

1312 *on sted of yowr helme* (on the surface of your helmet). MS reads *in* for *on*. A *bugyl* is a buffalo, ox, or young bull. Line 1353 indicates that the *bugyl* is a sculpted or painted image of the animal, and line 1489 suggests it is probably a helmet crest. See also line 1369. Such heraldic crests, initially for the purposes of identification in tournaments, began to be used in the early fourteenth century and became extravagant pieces of decoration. Depictions in art, such as the Manasseh Codex (c. 1300–30) from Germany and funeral effigies like that of Richard Beauchamp, earl of Warwick (d. 1439) in St. Mary's Church, Warwick, attest to the long and widespread use of such devices. (See, for example, Maurice Keen, *Chivalry* [New Haven: Yale University Press, 1984], pp. 17, 18, 22, and 36). Why the *bugyl* should be *gapyng* is not clear, but an ox-like animal is the crest of the Yorkshire Methams. According to Trevisa, the *bugyl* is either black or red, and its milk "is ful good ageins smytynge of serpente" (2:1151).

1313 According to the lapidaries the *carbunkyl* (carbuncle), or ruby, is one of the twelve precious stones that God named to Moses, consequently signifying the second of the Ten Commandments, and is said to have been in the River of Paradise. It is held to be the most virtuous of stones, according honor to those who possess it and comforting the anguished who look upon it. Sick animals that drink water in which a ruby has been immersed will be made well. It is likened to a burning coal, and because of its gleaming brightness, it is said to light the darkness and therefore signifies Jesus Christ.

1314 Cleopes' gifts are reminiscent of Medea's gifts to Jason in Gower's *Confessio Amantis* V.3559–3622 and in Lydgate's *Troy Book* (I.2988 ff.). Medea gives Jason a ring, a silver image, a vial of liquid to protect him against the oxen and serpent that guard the Golden Fleece. Medea's knowledge of the liberal arts, necromancy, illusions, astronomy, so eloquently popularized by Gower and Lydgate, perhaps provided Metham with some inspiration for his heroine's character.

      ylke. MS: *yche*. The scribe makes the same mistake in reading his exemplar in line 1641.

1315 The lapidaries treat the *smaragdus*, or emerald, in some detail. They point out, for example, that the Apocalypse of St. John identifies the emerald as the fourth foundation stone of the New Jerusalem, Heaven, and therefore it signifies the four Evangelists of the New Testament. By similar allegorical interpretations, it also symbolizes true faith and the Trinity. Emerald is the greenest of all green things, and is also one of the stones found in the River of Paradise, located in Syria. It has a number of medicinal purposes and moral significations, and encourages one to be chaste and to love good works.

1320   *orytes*, also called *corinth* in the lapidaries, protects its bearer from the venomous bites of evil beasts or adders, and attacks by other wild animals in the wilderness. It also causes infertility and miscarriages in humans.

1321   *third.* MS: *iii.*

1321–22 The lapidaries identify *ligure*, or *lyncurium*, as stone from India that is engendered in river gravel and protected or hidden by the lynx or the ox. The oxen that tills the ground and hides the stone signifies the preparation of Christ's land, which is tilled by holy prophecy and good preachers. God gave this stone many virtues: it cures jaundice, gout, and staunches bleeding wounds; it makes lecherous men chaste. *Demonius* is mentioned in Vincent of Beauvais' *Speculum Naturale* as a stone that counteracts poison (Craig, p. 169). Although the lapidaries treat *Agapys* (also called *agatten*) and *acates* as different minerals, they appear to be variant terms for *agate*. The two stones share the common property of being a remedy against the sting of scorpions and the bite of serpents. The *Peterborough Lapidary* indicates that *agapys* should be ingested with white wine.

1325   Mugwort (*Modyrwort*) is a plant formerly thought to have medicinal value; rue (*rwe*) is "a perennial evergreen shrub . . . having bitter, strong scented leaves which were formerly much used for medicinal purposes" (OED), and Trevisa writes that serpents hate the smell of rue, which inhibits their ability to flee (2:1132); red mallow (*red malwys*) is a variety of mallow with a dark crimson flower; mountain calamynt (*calamynt mownteyn*) is a "genus of aromatic herbs," which according to Turner's *Herbal* (1568) "is good for them that ar byten of serpentes" (OED).

1326   For *Orygannum*, see above, line 1284. Trevisa writes that seed of fennel (*fenel*), if "ydronk with wyne helpith ageins bytyng of serpentes and styngyng of scorpiouns" (2:960). Dragon's wort (*dragannys*), named for its speckled stalk, is supposedly like the coloration of serpent's skin; if the juice of this plant is ingested or used as a balm, it drives away serpents with its smell (Trevisa, 2:943; see also OED, *dragon*, 14).

1360   MS: extraneous *s* before *same*; so too on *stedfastenes*, line 2099.

1362   A proverbial expression; see Whiting, W389 and W45.

1371   *besechyng*. MS: *besechyn*.

1379   *and wyth*. MS: *and a with*.

1383   *honesté*. MS: *honeste oneste*.

1420   *schynyng*. MS: *schynyg*.

1423   *phylatery*. Amoryus' potion used "for the cure of venomous diseases" (OED 2, *Blancard's Physical Dictionary*, 1693). See also the note to lines 169–75.

1435   *reisyd*. MS: *reisysyd*.

1438   *Schuld . . . devour*. MS: *Schul . . . devouryd*.

1442   *sqwyftly*. MS: *qwyftly*.

1454   MS: *e* written above the *a* in *slayn*.

1462   MS: extraneous *c* after *ye*.

1464   MS duplicates *odyr*, the second marked for deletion.

1470   Craig places the phrase *And on the goddys alle* on a separate but unnumbered line, giving the appearance of an eight-line stanza. In the MS, the phrase follows directly after *falle* on the same line.

1471   *Sche*. MS: *che*.

1487   *I may this wrytyng on the phylysophyr vouche*. Metham is apparently referring to some bestiary or encyclopedic work.

1491   *confusde*. MS: *confude*.

1493–94 A proverbial expression; see Whiting, S408 and S409.

1506   *glyde*. "Said of the mode of progression of reptiles" (OED 2).

1512 *Hys brystylyd mosel gan blwe wer as ony led*. His bristled muzzle became as blue as lead. *blwe*: "livid, leaden-colored" (OED, *blue* 2).

1517–19 MS: *Fyl doune that as an erthen the ground schake*. Craig emends *schake* to *quake* so that the rhyme word in line 1519 will not be duplicated, but the syntax is still corrupt. I have emended the rhyme word of line 1519 from the MS reading of *schake* to *qwake*. The poet himself *qwake[s] for fere* twice (lines 1568 and 1657).

1531 *wundyr*. MS: *wyth undyr*; *to* supplied.

1535 *mynstrelsy*. Minstrels were primarily musicians, but they also provided other kinds of entertainment, including singing, dancing, and the recitation of poetry. Medieval documents indicate that minstrels did at times accompany various processions.

1541 *lyvys*. MS: *lyverys*.

1545 *memoratyf dart*, that is, Cupid's dart or arrow, calling to mind his love.

1549 *veneryan*. "Venereal," pertaining to sexual desire (OED, *venerian* 2). MS: *flamme*.

1556 MS: *That*. Craig emends to *Than*.

1560 *Orphe*. See notes to lines 549–52.

1562 *Parys*. Paris, the son of the Trojan king Priam; Paris' abduction of Helen from the Greeks led to the destruction of Troy by the Greeks and his own death. Various versions of the Troy story were widely circulated in Latin, French, and English versions in the Middle Ages. At least part of John Lydgate's *Troy Book* was familiar to Metham, and Chaucer's *Troilus and Criseyde* served in a number of ways as a model for *Amoryus and Cleopes* (see Introduction).

1564 Metham here invokes the inexpressibility topos, a commonplace of medieval rhetoric. The words *rhetorician* or *rhetoric* were often used to praise Chaucer in the fifteenth century and consequently may also be equated with our notion of *poet* or *poetry*.

1584 *redres*. The verb had a number of senses available in the fifteenth century, some now obsolete. Among these are "to direct or address (a thing) to a destination or in specified course" (OED 5); "to cure, heal, relieve (a disease, wound, etc.)" (OED

10.b); and "to rise, to become erect" (OED 1.c). Metham then may be alluding to the "disease" of love's sickness as well as creating a *double entendre*.

1589   MS reads *ther speke* with a canceled *e* above the *th-*, and the *speke* changed to *speche*.

1590   *qwyle*. MS: *qwylk*.

1593   A reference to the doctrine of God's foreknowledge of all events, widely disseminated from Boethius' *Consolation of Philosophy*, Books 4 and 5.

1596   *systyrrys sevyn*. Sisters seven, that is, the star system of the Pleiades.

1598   Marginal note: *Qwat a lemyng sterre betokynnyth qwan tho apperyth.*

1603   *same morw*. MS: *same agan morw*, with *agan* marked for cancellation.

1606   *posterin yate* is a private or rear entrance, distinct from the main gate.

1614   *chas*. A chase is "a tract of unenclosed land reserved for breeding and hunting wild animals" or simply "unenclosed park land" (OED).

1621   *hyinde* is a female deer, after its third year.

1626   *kerchyf* is from the French *couvrechef*. The early twelfth-century romance of *Piramus et Tisbé* and the *Ovide Moralisé* use the word *guymple*; its English form is *wimple*, used by Chaucer in his version of the story in *The Legend of Good Women*. Metham's version of the poem has derived from second and later textual tradition that uses the more fashionable article of clothing, the *kerchyff*.

1632   MS has *c* changed to a *k*.

1642   *desteny*. MS: *dyesteny*, with superscript first *e*.

1643   MS has *thei wyth* changed to *ther*.

1645   *ony*. MS: *in*.

1646   Craig incorrectly numbers this line as 1645. Corresponding line numbers in this edition will therefore differ from those in his until line 2084, for which, see below.

1655   *espys*. The genitive of *asp*, a tree of the poplar family, "the leaves of which are specially liable to tremulous motion" (OED).

1663   *conseyt*. "A (morbid) affection or seizure of the body or mind" (OED).

1664   *mornyng*. MS: *mornyg*.

        hys. MS: *ys*.

1665   *most trw* is repeated and canceled.

1676   *hert*. A hart is a male red deer.

1679   *Companeus* is a chief in the Greek army at the siege of Troy. He boasted that even Zeus could not stop him from gaining his objective. Chaucer writes in the *Troilus*: "Capaneus the proude / With thonder-dynt was slayn, that cride loude" (V.1504–05). MS reads *slow ca Companeus* with *ca* canceled.

1684   Marginal note: *Pluto god of helle and erthe*.

1685–86 *Amphyorax* knew he would die if he went to the siege at Thebes, so he hid, only to be revealed by his wife. At the siege, he is swallowed up by the earth. Chaucer refers to the story several times (see, for example, *Troilus* V.1500), and Lydgate narrates Amphyorax's demise in his *Siege of Thebes* (3:4023–84), where he goes to Hell for his idolotry and necromancy. The fact that *Amoryus and Cleopes* refers to both Campaneus and Amphyorax in such close proximity, as does Chaucer in the *Troilus*, suggests Metham might have had a copy of Chaucer's work at hand, perhaps through the Earl of Suffolk, who had a number of Chaucer manuscripts in his keeping.

1698   MS duplicates and marks for cancellation a second *alone* after *wrecche*.

1698–99 In Book IV of the *Metamorphoses*, the same book where the story of Pyramus and Thisbe occurs, Ovid relates the story of Juno's travels to the underworld seeking the three *Furyis*, sister goddesses of vengeance, who viciously attack those guilty of some breach of kinship obligations. Amoryus' use of the word *onkend* (unkind) —

meaning unnatural, wicked, unfilial, undutiful, or faithless — in line 1705 alludes to obligations of kinship; Cleopes uses the same word in a similar context (line 1750). Juno also encounters *Cerberus*, the three-headed dog (hence Metham's *Tricerberus*) that guards the entrance to the Hell.

1700   *thow*. Craig reads *yow*, but the letter is clearly an old-style thorn, not the scribe's typical y-shaped letter that can be either *y* or thorn.

1711–15 Metham's use of anaphora echoes a favorite device of Chaucer. See *Troilus* V.1828ff. and V.1849ff.

1717   *pomel*. A pommel is the knob at the end of the hilt of the sword.

1752   *O, Saturne*. In the epilogue to *Troilus* (V.1809) most Chaucer manuscripts locate Troilus' placement after his death in the seventh sphere. Modern editors prefer the eighth sphere, since that is where Arcite goes in Boccaccio's *Teseide*, which is Chaucer's source for that passage and which seems a more likely place if Troilus is to look down on earth "with ful avysement" (V.1811). But it is almost certain that any manuscript of *Troilus and Criseyde* that Metham might have seen would have read "seventh sphere" (i.e., Saturn's sphere) and thus the place and the patron Cleopes would invoke in her desire to join her lover in the sphere where Saturn might him *deyfy* (line 1753).

1753   *spere* (sphere). See above the notes to line 279 and lines 304–10.

1754   *soulys leche*, soul's physician, a common epithet for Christ.

1759   MS reads *sey*, with superscript *a* above the *e*.

1763   *nede*. "These dire circumstances," but the sense may suggest Cleopes' obligation to act (OED I.9 and II.12).

1770   *eld tyme paynymmys yt dyd for a memoryal*. It is conceivable that Metham gets his idea for rejecting the cursed pagan rite from Chaucer's epilogue to *Troilus* (esp. V.1849–53), where Chaucer then turns to a Christain theogony for his conclusion.

1773–78 The excuse for lack of finesse in writing was commonplace in the later Middle Ages, but Metham here excuses his lack of rhetorical skills by employing one, the *occupatio*.

1782   *synderesys.* "The faculty of the mind which judges and recommends moral conduct" (MED).

1783   *oryens sol justycye.* "the rising sun of justice," an epithet for Christ, with the commonplace pun on sun/Son and the allusion to His rising at the Resurrection. In this prologue, the narrator turns to a Christian muse rather than the classical ones invoked earlier.

1790   Craig reads *Adamyrgyk*, for which he suggests "Adam's servitude" based on a tenuous etymological connection. What Craig sees as an *r* is really a ligature of the recurved tail of the first *y* and scribe's punctuation mark, which looks like a modern colon. A similar ligature of a letter with a recurved tail and the punctuation mark occurs in line 1793. An abbreviation stroke above the *m*, which usually signals an *m* or *n*, may be employed here to indicate the *s*.

1791   After the Crucifixion, Heaven became open to the souls of the righteous, who before were automatically confined to Hell because of Adam's sin. In the Harrowing of Hell following the Crucifixion, Christ confronted Satan, and forced the release of the righteous, who then accompanied him to Heaven.

1803   *lyvyth.* MS: *lyvyh.*

        wyth spyryte or grennes. Perhaps the sense is "whether animated or vegetable," but the sense is difficult. Two forms of life seem to be the point.

1807a   *[Here Endyth the Prolog and Begynnyth the Laste Boke].* The heading does not appear in the MS, but the word *Amoryus* in the next line begins with a 2-line-high capital letter as the text turns from invocation to narration.

1809   *Ore.* Suggested by the Latin verb *orare*, meaning *to speak oratorically, to pray*.

1810   *hermyte.* According to Jacques Le Goff, "The model holy man was the isolated hermit, the man who in the eyes of the lay masses truly realized the solitary ideal, and who was the highest manifestation of the Christian ideal" (*Medieval Civilization 400–1500*, trans. Julia Barrow [London: Blackwell, 1988], p. 184); a number of hermits were elevated to sainthood. Fictional hermits appear in many *chansons de geste* and romances, including the French *Yvain*, the German *Parsifal*, and the English *Guy of Warwick* and *Stanzaic Morte Arthur*.

1853–55 Mary's role as an intercessor on behalf of sinners to save them from God's damnation was a key one and greatly contributed to the widespread and sanctioned cult of the Virgin in the later Middle Ages.

1863 Marginal note: *How the ermyght reysyd Amoryus and Cl[e]opes fro deth to lyffe.*

1866 *And thow I be noght wurthy of my merytys.* The hermit is referring to the theological doctrine of merits, which posits that good works entitle a person to a reward from God. His assertion that he is not worthy and lacks merit demonstrates his humility rather than any want of goodness.

1867 *wemme.* In addition to meaning "injury" (OED 2), *wem* can also mean "scar" (OED 3) or "moral defilement; (stain of sin)" (OED 1). In the case of Amoryus and Cleopes, the last sense would apply to the absolution of the mortal sin of suicide. Also, the lovers later prove their resurrection by showing their scars.

1871 *voys.* MS: *voy.*

1875–76 *Salve . . . regina mater misericordye.* The first line of a famous medieval antiphon sung at compline, the last canonical office of the day. This antiphon was also the subject of sermons and other hymns, and appeared in Books of Hours.

1877 *qwene and modyr of mercy.* Commonplace epithets for Mary, who was often referred of as Queen of Heaven, and who, because of her intercessory role, was often appealed to for mercy. The spontaneous singing of the Marian anthem places the story of resurrection of the lovers within a large body of medieval tales in which the Virgin intercedes for sinners, including suicides. See, for example, "The Good Knight and his Jealous Wife," in Beverly Boyd, ed., *The Middle English Miracles of the Virgin* (San Marino, CA: The Huntington Library, 1964), pp. 92–104.

1888 *memoryal.* MS: *memoryl.*

1898 At the end of this line the MS reads *and.* As the start of line 1899 begins with *And,* I have omitted the apparently superfluous *and* in line 1898.

1906 *faryth as a feyre, ever onstabyl* echoes *Troilus* V.1840–41: "and thynketh al nys but a faire, / This world that passeth soone as floures faire."

1909 *thise transytory thingys onstabyl.* See note to lines 387–88.

Notes

1910–11 This is a paraphrase of Matthew 19:22–23.

1922   *But vertuus love of God was never denyid.* The ideas of virtuous heathens receiving grace despite their alien birth is popular from the later fourteenth century on. See, for example, the salvation of Trajan in *Piers Plowman* B 11.135–67 and B 12.210ff., and in *The Trentals of St Gregory*; see also the elaborate salvation of the virtuous pagan lawyer in *St. Erkenwald.*

1929   *thinkyth yow.* The impersonal verb with its object, addressed to Cleopes in the polite plural.

1933   *Wele.* MS: *Wwele.*

1936   *haruyd helle.* See above the note to line 1791.

1961   MS reads *Qhan*, canceled; *Than* added in the margin.

1981   An awkward stroke above *ye* suggests some scribal hesitancy about whether the form *yen* or *ye*, the one representing the plural elsewhere, the latter supplying a correct rhyme.

1982   *Wyth.* The only instance of the non-abbreviated form of the preposition in the poem. This spelling is common in other manuscripts from Norfolk.

1987   Marginal note: *How the hermyght destroyid the image off Venus.*

1993   *mankend.* MS: *manked.*

        mansyon. The word has astrological significance, related to the domicile of a planet. See note to line 305.

2011   Marginal note: *How the hermyght dyssolvyd the spere.*

2015   *envye.* MS: *evye.*

2022   *as the smoke of a fere* is proverbial; see Whiting, S414.

2029   *krystyn.* MS: *kyrstyn.*

2031   This is the first time in the poem that the temple is referred to as a church.

2039   *fulfyllyd.* MS: *fulfully.*

2046   A proverbial phrase; see Whiting, M695.

2054   *Cleopes.* MS: *Clopes.* So too in line 2082.

2066   Marginal note: *How Amorius and Cleopes wre mariid.*

2078   *prosperyté.* MS: properyte. So too in line 2117.

2084   Craig misnumbers this line 2085. The discrepancy between the numbering of lines in Craig's edition and in this one, begun at line 1646, is thus resolved here.

2087   MS reads *Clopes,* but Craig incorrectly emends to *Cloepes.* Marginal note: *How Amoryus and Cleopes dyid and were byryid togydyr.*

2092   *wrytyn.* MS: *wrytys.*

2094   *Flowre of knyghthod* is a proverbial epithet; see Whiting, F311

2106   *eldtyme.* MS: *heldtyme.*

2113   *hundred and two.* MS: *cii.* An "l," perhaps for Roman numeral 50, has been added above *cii.* Why this particular length of time was chosen is unclear, but if the figure 102 is intended, that would indicate the year 1346/1347, and perhaps allude to the famous English victory against the French at Crécy in France. On the date of the composition of this poem, see the note to line 2177 below.

2122–23 Proverbial; see Whiting, T464, and above note to lines 55–56.

2126   *fyfty.* MS: *l.*

2128   *he ys an hole reme to have in governauns.* The narrator ascribes the same ability to Amoryus in line 98.

2129–31 *Sapyens* is the apocryphal *Book of Wisdom,* attributed to Solomon. Metham is referring to *Wisd* 8:6–7, "And if prudence worke; who of all that is a more cunning

130

workeman than [Wisdom]?" The first line may also allude to *Proverbs* 24:27, also attributed to Solomon.

2136 *Waxham*, a town on the Norfolk Broads, near Stapleton's manor at Ingham.

  Gyldenerrys are Flemings. There were a number of Fleming enclaves in Norfolk in the fifteenth century, and there were often tensions between the English and these "foreigners," mainly engaged in cloth manufacture and mercantile trade, the primary industry of late medieval East Anglia.

2138 MS reads *thei* in the text, but *the* is added in the margin.

2139 *King Cassyon* is unknown.

2141 *Corbellyon*. Craig suggests *Corbeil*, a town in northern France which was occupied by English forces during the Hundred Years War.

2144 *Alexander Macedo*. That is, Alexander (the Great) of Macedon. Chaucer mentions "Alixandre Macedo" in his *House of Fame* (line 915), referring to an episode in Alexander romances in which Alexander voyages through the heavens. Metham's reference may refer to a complete Alexander romance, not just the celestial voyage. Literature relating to Alexander was among the most popular and widespread in the late Middle Ages.

2145 *Josue* is probably Joshua, Moses' successor who led the Israelites into the Promised land. See Exodus 17:9; Numbers 27:18–23; and Joshua 1–24.

  Josepus could refer to any of a number of medieval romances or histories, including the story of Joseph of Arimathea, or perhaps the "Forray de Gadderis," the first part of the Middle Scots *Buik of Alexander* (1438 AD) by Sir Gilbert Hay, which takes place in the Vale of Josephus. Another possibility is that it refers to the story of Flavius Josephus, a Jewish historian who commanded the Israelites in a war with the Romans (66 AD). Chaucer refers to this Josephus in the *House of Fame* (3:1429-40). None of these works by Metham has survived.

2150–56 Katherine Stapleton, Sir Miles' second wife, was the first cousin of William de la Pole, Duke of Suffolk (see the Introduction).

2155   *markeys*. Marquis is a title of the peerage between those of earl and duke. William had been the chief advisor to Henry VI during the 1440s; he was murdered in 1450, apparently not long after *Amoryus and Cleopes* was written.

2170   *Crysaunt* is another of Metham's lost works. It is possibly a translation of Petrus de Crescentiis' (1233–c. 1320) *De Omnibus Agriculturae Partibus et Plantarium Animalique*, an encyclopedia of farming and raising livestock. Although such a work would have been useful for a large landowner like Stapleton, it is unlike the other narratives that Metham claims to have written.

2172   *degré*. MS: *dregre*.

2173   *qwene Eleyne*. Helen of Troy, whom Chaucer mentions in several of his works and whose beauty was a medieval commonplace. *Cresseyd* is Chaucer's heroine in *Troilus and Criseyde*. A much longer list of exemplary women occurs in a poem ascribed to Lydgate, "The Floure of Curtesy," deriving from the *Balade* in the *Prologue* to *The Legend of Good Women*. See *The Minor Poems of John Lydgate*, ed. Henry Noble MacCracken, EETS o.s. 192 (1934; rpt. Oxford: Oxford University Press, 1961), pp. 440–48.

2174   *Polyxchene* is Polyxena, one of King Priam's daughters. Chaucer's Troilus compares the three women, thinking that Criseyde "fairer was to sene / Than evere were Eleyne or Polixene" (I.454–55). *Grysyld* is Griselde, the heroine of The Clerk's Tale, who is praised for her "vertuous beautee" (line 211) and especially for her patience in suffering the outrageous trials of her husband. *Penelopé*, the wife of Odysseus, is mentioned in several of Chaucer's works as a model of fidelity. Craig (p. 163) argues on the basis of these two lines that Metham did not know Chaucer's works well, but his argument is based in part on Skeat's edition of Chaucer.

2177   *the sevyn and twenty yere of the sext Kyng Henry*. MS: *xxvii*. The twenty-seventh year of King Henry VI's reign, that is, 1448/49; "but Metham is probably using the regnal dates, as was common, to refer to the calendar year 1449" (Derek Pearsall, *John Lydgate* [London: Routledge, 1970], p. 299n7).

2178   *Go now, lytyl boke* is modeled on Chaucer's famous phrase *Go, litel bok, go* at the end of his *Troilus* (V.1786). Verbatim borrowings from and variations on Chaucer's expression were commonplace among fifteenth-century English poems.

2183   *undyr correccion.* "subject to correction." Chaucer's Parson puts his "meditation" under the correction of other clerics (line 60), and the narrator of the *Troilus* subjects his words to the correction of lovers as they see fit (III.1331–35). This subjection to superiors, a form of the humility topos, was a widespread motif in fifteenth-century poems.

2193   *Jon Lydgate* was a monk at the important Abbey of St. Edumund, Bury St. Edmunds, Suffolk. He was one of the most prodigious and most influential writers of the fifteenth century. The word *sumtyme* and line 2199 indicates that Metham knew of Lydgate's death which occurred in 1449.

2195   *half chongyd Latyne* (half-changed Latin), referring to Lydgate's aureate diction.

2213–22 Craig observed in his edition that there were ten lines erased at the end of the manuscript. The use of ultraviolet light now makes these last ten lines of the manuscript partially visible. Because of a careful erasure and a thin vellum, some portions of the deletion are still illegible. The erased lines follow directly on the preceding stanza, as is typical in the manuscript; but the ten lines violate the seven-line rhyme royal scheme of the poem, perhaps providing a rationale for the erasure, although some reader may simply have objected to Metham's autobiographical conclusion. See the Introduction.

2219   *Decendyd.* MS: *Decedyd.*

Appendix

Pierre Bersuire's Metamorphosis Ovidiana Moraliter . . . Explanata

The Story of Piramus and Thisbe[1]

Piramus was the most handsome young man and Thisbe the most beautiful maiden in the city of Babylon, where they lived in adjacent houses. They loved one another intensely, but because of others, they were unable to express their ideas to one another except by conversing through a fissure in a wall. Consequently, in order that they might be able to be united, they agreed that they would leave their fathers' houses that night and meet outside of the city at the tomb of Ninus, under a certain mulberry tree next to an icy-cold fountain. There they might relieve themselves of love's pain. This agreement delighted them, but the sun seemed to depart slowly until finally it plunged beneath the seas and the night rushed up. In brief, the girl — whom love made foolhardy, inflamed by passion — arrived first at the cenotaph of Ninus and sat under the tree as agreed. Lo, a thirsty lioness comes to the foresaid fountain and lies down. Seeing the beast, Thisbe, frightened by the dreadful thing, fled on timid feet into a dark cave in order to hide. However, in fleeing, a ribbon fell from her dress, and the lion, having come upon it, bloodied the ribbon with its bloodstained maw and tore the thin garment to shreds.

Going out later, Piramus comes to the fountain under the mulberry after the lioness had drunk from the fountain and returned to the forest; and discovering Thisbe's bloody ribbon, he thus reasonably concludes that she has been devoured by wild beasts and had to be dead, entirely consumed. Grieving and beating his chest in sorrow, he says, "One night destroys two lovers!" Declaring this and a great many other lamentations in this place, and armed, he impaled his side with his own iron sword, stabbed himself. So, in this way, his dying blood, spewing out high, changed the mulberry fruit, which was white, to a dark color; and the roots, soaked with blood, tinged the hanging berries with a purple hue. Thisbe, then coming to the fountain after being driven away by dread of the lioness, which by this time had disappeared from view, is astonished by the darkened fruit of the

---

[1] Translated from the Latin facsimile edition, ed. Stephen Orgel (1509; rpt., New York: Garland, 1979).

135

tree. She finds Piramus pierced by his own sword and determines that to have been done because of his passion. She took up the sword of Piramus, who by this time was cooled by death, and stabbed herself and, along with her lover, terminated her own life.

In the light of day, their parents became acquainted with the revelations, and then the bodies of those two were cremated together and the ashes placed in the same urn.

This story can be taken as an allegory of the Passion and Incarnation of Christ. Piramus is the son of God, and Thisbe, the human spirit, both of which from the very beginning had chosen each other. Through benevolent love and a passionate desire to be joined together, they wished to become as one.[2] Because they were side by side as it were, alike in all respects, man was made in God's image. However, a certain wall — that is, the sin of Adam — was separating those two and impeding their union. Spontaneously, according to the prophets' commentaries, they had agreed to meet through the blessed Incarnation and under the fruit tree, that is, under the cross, and mutually to intermingle at the fountain of baptism and grace. So, therefore, it happened that the girl, the human spirit, was not able to approach the fountain of grace on account of the lion, which is the devil. But Piramus, who is God, waited in silence for the arrival of his friend. *Habakkuk* 2:3: "Though it tarry, wait for it, because it will surely come, it will not tarry." Therefore, the One, fixed in his purpose, came to us as agreed, and exposed himself to death under the tree of the cross because of the love of Thisbe, who is the soul. So, he bloodied that very tree — clearly the cross — and darkened its color.

And Thisbe, who is the faithful soul, is bound by her compassion to stab herself with the sword of the Passion and mindfully to sustain the same punishment. Actually, that girl is the Virgin Mary, to whom the Son of God came by the Incarnation and was willing to die on the tree of the cross. She in truth stabbed herself with the sword because of her compassion. *Luke* 2:35: "A sword shall pierce through my own soul."

---

[2] The passage employs two pairs of nouns to underscore the gender difference and the anthropomorphic union of the two entities: *son* and *passionate desire* are both masculine, *spirit* and *charity* are both feminine.

Glossary

a (article) *a*; (interjection) *ah*; (v.) *have*; **an** (pl.) *have*

af(f)tyr *after, according to*

alle *all*

and *and, if*

anone *immediately*

ansqwer *answer*

aspye, asspye *espy*

astoynyd *astonished*

autor, autour *author*

ayen, ayeyn(e) *again, in return, in reply, back [to a place or state], against*

ayen(s) *against, facing toward, before, in the presence of*

bare (v.) *bore* (p.t. of bear); (adj.) *barren*

batayl(e), batel, bateyl *battle*

be (inf. and subj.) *be*; (pres. pl.) *are*; (p.p.) *been*

be *by; with*

befforn, beforn *before*

ben(e) (p.p.) *been*

bere (n.) *bear*; (v.) *bear*

best (adj.) *best*; (n.) *beast*

beute *beauty*

blyssyd *blessed, rejoiced*

boke *book*

broute, browt(e) *brought*

bugyl *ox, young bull*

bysyly *with fixed attention, assiduously, energetically, diligently*

case *case, matter, situation, event, occurrence, chance*

certen, certeyn(e), certyn *certain*

chauns *that which befalls a person; chance, fortune, luck; an unexpected or unforeseen event; an occurrence beyond human control, fate, destiny*

chere *face, countenance, expression, mood, demeanor*

clepe *call, name*

clepyd *called, named*

clerk, -ys *member of the clergy, scholar*

compleyn(e) *to express sorrow, grief, or suffering, especially in matters of love; to lament*

conseyt *conceit, idea, faculty of understanding, personal opinion; work of art*

coud(e) *could*

crany *hole, crack, fissure*

creature *any created being; person*

cuntré *country; region*

cyté *city*

cyteceyn *citizen*

dar(e) *dare*

ded(e) *dead; deed*

deme *think, suppose, determine*

dere (adj.) *dear, beloved, costly;* (v.) *to injure, harm*

despousyd *married*

doth(e), dotht *does*

drw(e) *drew*

dye, dyid *die, died*

dyght *adorned, prepared*

eke *also*

eld(e) *old*

endyght(e), endyt(e) *to write, to compose [a poem, etc.], to describe*

erbe, pl. erbys *herbs*

erbere *arbor*

er(h)myght, ermyt(e) *hermit, anchorite*

erly *early*

erth(e), ertht *earth*

erth(e)ly *earthly*

este *east*

evyn (n.) *evening;* (adv.) *exactly, precisely, "just"*

eyen *eyes*

fadyr, fader *father*

falle (v.) *fall; befall, happen*

feld (n.) *field;* (v. p.p.) *knocked down*

felycyte *happiness*

fend *fiend, the Devil*

fer *far*

fere (n.) *fear;* (v.) *to fear*

fers *fierce*

fersly *fiercely*

feyth *faith*

foreby, forby *close by, near; past*

forsayd, forseyd (p.p.) *aforesaid*

fresch *young, vigorous, blooming, lovely*

fro *from*

ful, full(e) (adj.) *full; complete;* (adv.) *completely, very;* **at the ful** *completely*

fygure *form, image, illustration; astrological sign, constellation*

fyl(e), fylle (v. p.t.) *fell; befell*

fyre *fire*

fyry *fiery*

fyrmament *sky, heavens, celestial sphere*

gan (to) *began; did;* (the periphrastic past tense) *(*e.g., **gan calle**: *called, did call;* **gan to syng**: *sang, did sing)*

glyde *pass over a surface;* (of weapons), *making a swift unrestrained blow; to pierce the heart;* (of reptiles), *a smoother motion*

goddes, godys *goddess*

goddessys *goddesses*

goddys, goddis, goddyis *gods*

godely goodely (adj.) *kind, fair, comely;* (adv.) *courteously, with propriety, liberally*

goulys *red*

governaus *manner of governing; rule; wise self-control, demeanor*

gret(e) *great*

gretly *greatly*

harnes (n.) *defensive armor for man or war horse, weaponry;* (v.) *to arm*

hart *heart; stag*

hast *haste;* (2nd pers. sing., pres.) *have*

hat, hath(e) (3rd pers. sing., pres.) *has*

hed *head*

hem *them, themselves*

herd *hard; heard*

her(e) *hear; here; their; her*

hert *heart; stag*
hertys *hearts*
ho *who*
hole *whole*
hom(e) *whom; home*
hos *whose*
hy(e) (n.) *haste;* (v.) *hasten;* (adv.) *immediately;* (adj.) *high*
hym *him*
hys *his*

iche *each*
in fere *together, in company*

juberté *jeopardy*
jurney, jurny *journey*
just(e) (pl. justys) *joust*

kerchyf(f) *a cloth used to cover the head, breast, neck or shoulders*
knw(e) *knew*
knyght, knygt (pl. knyghtys, knytys) *knight*
kyst *cast*

lere, lern(e) *teach, instruct*
let(e), lett (forms for present and past tenses are alike) *let; permit; cease, stop, refrain; hinder; cause to be, cause to have*
let pase *let pass, discontinue*
lettyng *delay, hindrance*
leve (n.) *leave;* (v.) *leave, put aside; believe* (aphetic form)
lovys *loves, love's*
lyfe, lyffe *life*
lynage *lineage, family*
lyon, lyoun *lion*

lytyl *little*

maner *manner, way, kind of*
manful, manfful, manffyl *courageous, brave*
masynger *messenger*
mayer, mayre *mayor*
mend(e) *mind*
ment *imagined, intended*
mervel (n. and v.) *marvel*
mervulus *marvelous*
mevyng *moving*
mone *moon; moan, complaint, lament*
morw, morow, morwgh *morning*
mych(e) *much*
myry *merry*

nas *was not*
nede (n.) *need, crisis;* (adj.) *necessary*
nedys (adv.) *necessarily*
ner *nor*
nere *near*
nest(e) *next*
noght, nowght, nowt (n.) *nothing;* (adv.) *not*
noudyr, nowdyr *neither*
nwe *new*

odyr, owdyr (pron.) *other(s), the other;* (adj.) *other*
off *of; by; for; concerning*
offt(e), offtyn *often*
on *on, to, in* (**on this wise / maner** *in this way*)
ony *any*
onys *once*
or (conj.) *or, before*
owre *our*

Glossary

owt(e) *out*

pase *pass*
payd *pleased, satisfied*
paynym(m)ys *heathens*
pepyl *people*
Perse *Persia*
peyn *pain, anguish, torment, suffering, punishment*
pleasauns, pleasuns, plesauns *pleasure, amusement, delight*
prayere, prayur, prayyer(e), preyur, preyyer *prayer*
preve *turn out*
privy *secret, hidden, personal*
puryfye *purify, refine*

quod *said*
qwan *when*
qwat *what*
qwedyr, qwydyr, qwyder *whether*
qwer(e), quere *where*
qwerf(f)or(e) *wherefore, for which reason*
qwy *why*
qwych(e) *which;* **the qwych(e)** *who, which*
qwyght, qwyte *white*
qwyle, qwylys *while*
qwyt(e) *pay back in revenge; conduct one's self* (with reflexive pronoun)

red(e) *red; read*
redres *redress, amend*
redy *ready*
regyon *region, country*
reherse *narrate, repeat, tell, relate, describe*

reme *realm, kingdom*
remembrauns, remenbrauns *memory; recollection; memorial; token*
reule *rule*
right noght *not at all*
rude *rough, ignorant, unlearned*
ryght, rygt (adj.) *right (as opposed to left); direct, legitimate (in respect to lineage); true;* (adv. as an intensive) *precisely, exactly; very*
ryse *rise*

sapyens *wisdom*
sayd *said*
sche *she*
schew(e) *show*
schewyd *showed*
schul *shall*
se(e) *see; sea*
sey *saw; say*
seyd *said*
seyn *seen; say*
seyng *saying*
seyth(t) *says*
slayn(e) *slain*
sle(e) *slay*
smet (p.t. of **smite**) *struck [with a weapon or blow]; broke [by striking]*
soden *sudden, unforeseen, impetuous*
sodenly *suddenly*
solempnyté *formal ceremony; solemnity*
sone *son; soon, quickly*
sore (adj.) *sore, painful, sorrowful;* (adv.) *painfully, intensely, grievously, vigorously, bitterly*
spere *sphere; spear*
sqweete, sqwet(e) *sweet; melodious, harmonious*

Glossary

sqweme *grief, affliction, sorrow*

sqwemfful *grievous, sorrowful*

sqwemffuly *sorrowfully, grievously*

sqwerd *sword*

sqwych(e) *such*

stent *stint, completed task*

sterre *star*

sterrys *stars*

stod(e) *stood*

ston(e) (-ys) *stone, stones*

story(e), (-is) *story*

styrt *started, rose up suddenly, sprung up, moved swiftly, recoiled in surprise or alarm*

sum, summe *some*

sumtyme *formerly, once; sometimes*

sundry *various, diverse, manifold, several*

sythyn *since, since that time*

teld(e) *told*

thayr(e), theyr *their*

ther(e) *their, there*

thi, thin, thy, thyn (2nd pers. sing. genitive pron.; -n forms precede words with vowels) *thine (your)*

thise, thyse *these*

tho *those*

thought(e), thowt(e) *thought*

thow(e) (2nd pers. sing. nominative pron.) *thou (you); though*

thru *through*

thrw(e) *threw*

thys *this*

tokyn *token*

toune *town*

tresour, tresur *treasure*

trone *throne*

trost *trust*

trow(e) *believe, suppose, think*

trw(e) *true*

trwly *truly*

trwth(t)(e) *truth*

tungys *tongues, gossip*

tyl *until*

venym *venom, poison*

venymmus *venomous*

veryly *truly*

voys(e) *voice*

wal, walle *wall*

wele *well*

werk(e) *work*

werrour (-rys, -ys) werryur (-rys), weryour (-is) *warrior(s)*

wey *way*

wod(e) *crazy, angry*

wold *would*

wrowght, wrowgt, wrowt (p.t. and p.p. of *werk[e]*) *worked, wrought, made, created; proceeded; performed*

wryght, wryt(e) *write*

wrytyn *written*

wul, wol, wulle *will*

wurchyp (v.) *worship;* (n.) *worship, honor, renown*

wurthy *worthy*

wyse *manner, way; wise; construction*

wyt(e), wytt (v.) *know;* (n.) *intelligence, reason, great mental capacity*

wyth *with*

y *I*

yave *gave*

yche *each, every*

ydolatrerys *idolators*

ye *you*

yed(e) *went*

yeff, yeve *give*

yevyng *giving*

yf(f) *if*

yift *gift*

yit *yet*

yn *in*

yovyn *given*

yow(e) *you*

yowr(e) *your*

ys *is*

-ys, -is (n. pl.) *-s* (n. possesive and n. pl. possessive) *- 's, -s '*

yt *it*

Volumes in the Middle English Texts Series

The Floure and the Leafe, The Assemblie of Ladies, and *The Isle of Ladies,* ed. Derek Pearsall (1990)

Three Middle English Charlemagne Romances, ed. Alan Lupack (1990)

Six Ecclesiastical Satires, ed. James M. Dean (1991)

Heroic Women from the Old Testament in Middle English Verse, ed. Russell A. Peck (1991)

The Canterbury Tales: Fifteenth-Century Continuations and Additions, ed. John M. Bowers (1992)

Gavin Douglas, *The Palis of Honoure,* ed. David J. Parkinson (1992)

Wynnere and Wastoure and The Parlement of the Thre Ages, ed. Warren Ginsberg (1992)

The Shewings of Julian of Norwich, ed. Georgia Ronan Crampton (1993)

King Arthur's Death: The Middle English Stanzaic Morte Arthur and Alliterative Morte Arthure, ed. Larry D. Benson and Edward E. Foster (1994)

Lancelot of the Laik and Sir Tristrem, ed. Alan Lupack (1994)

Sir Gawain: Eleven Romances and Tales, ed. Thomas Hahn (1995)

The Middle English Breton Lays, ed. Anne Laskaya and Eve Salisbury (1995)

Sir Perceval of Galles and Ywain and Gawain, ed. Mary Flowers Braswell (1995)

Four Middle English Romances: Sir Isumbras, Octavian, Sir Eglamour of Artois, Sir Tryamour, ed. Harriet Hudson (1996)

The Poems of Laurence Minot (1333–1352), ed. Richard H. Osberg (1996)

Medieval English Political Writings, ed. James M. Dean (1996)

The Book of Margery Kempe, ed. Lynn Staley (1996)

Amis and Amiloun, Robert of Ciseyle, and Sir Amadace, ed. Edward E. Foster (1997)

The Cloud of Unknowing, ed. Patrick Gallacher (1997)

Robin Hood and Other Outlaw Tales, ed. Stephen Knight and Thomas H. Ohlgren (1997)

The Poems of Robert Henryson, ed. Robert Kindrick (1997)

Moral Love Songs and Laments, ed. Susanna Greer Fein (1998)

John Lydgate, *Troy Book: Selections,* ed. Robert R. Edwards (1998)

Thomas Usk, *The Testament of Love,* ed. R. Allen Shoaf (1998)

Prose Merlin, ed. John Conlee (1998)

Middle English Marian Lyrics, ed. Karen Saupe (1998)

Four Romances of England: King Horn, Havelok the Dane, Bevis of Hampton, Athelston, ed. Ronald B. Herzman, Graham Drake, and Eve Salisbury (1998)

John Metham, *Amoryus and Cleopes*, ed. Stephen F. Page (1999)

Other TEAMS Publications

Documents of Practice Series:

Love and Marriage in Late Medieval London, by Shannon McSheffrey (1995)

A Slice of Life: Selected Documents of Medieval English Peasant Experience, edited, translated, and with an introduction by Edwin Brezette DeWindt (1996)

Sources for the History of Medicine in Late Medieval London, by Carole Rawcliffe (1996)

Regular Life: Monastic, Canonical, and Mendicant Rules, selected with an introduction by Douglas J. McMillan and Kathryn Smith Fladenmuller (1997)

Commentary Series:

Commentary on the Book of Jonah, by Haimo of Auxere, translated with an introduction by Deborah Everhart (1993)

Medieval Exegesis in Translation: Commentaries on the Book of Ruth, translated with an introduction by Lesley Smith (1996)

Nicholas of Lyra's Apocalypse Commentary, translated with an introduction and notes by Philip D. W. Krey (1997)

Rabbi Ezra Ben Solomon of Gerona: Commentary on the Song of Songs and Other Kabbalistic Commentaries, selected, translated, and annotated by Seth Brody

To order please contact:

MEDIEVAL INSTITUTE PUBLICATIONS
Western Michigan University
Kalamazoo, MI 49008–3801
Phone (616) 387–8755
FAX (616) 387–8750

http://www.wmich.edu/medieval/mip/mipubshome/html